The Dilemma of Western Philosophy

This edited collection takes a multifaceted approach to the various limitations and achievements of Western philosophy. Considered on its own, Western philosophy is a highly contentious name. The contributors question its validity as a label and take to task its grand appearance within education. However, part of the problem with Western philosophy is that it has less conventional as well as dominant manifestations. The writers consider both forms of Western philosophy, devoting significant thought and time to it in its own right, but always referring it to the more specific issue of education. This book adds to a growing corpus that sketches the relationship between education and philosophy, showing that they are both deeply intertwined, and it is indeed philosophy (and especially its Western variation) that supports Western education and allows it to flourish in the first instance. It is fitting, then, that at various points this book depicts education as a hegemonic vehicle of a deeper phenomenon – that of dominant Western philosophy.

This book was originally published as a special issue of *Educational Philosophy and Theory*.

Michael A. Peters is Professor of Education at the University of Waikato, New Zealand. He is the Executive Editor of the journal *Educational Philosophy and Theory*. His interests are in education, philosophy and social policy, and he is the author of numerous books, including *The Global Financial Crisis and the Restructuring of Education* (with Besley, 2015), *Paulo Freire: The Global Legacy* (with Tina Besley, 2015) and *Education Philosophy and Politics: Selected Works* (2011).

Carl Mika is a senior lecturer in the Faculty of Education at University of Waikato, New Zealand. He is of Māori descent. He has a background in law practice, indigenous studies and aspects of Western philosophy. His current areas of research focus on indigenous colonial and counter-colonial theory, as well as philosophical research methods.

Educational Philosophy and Theory

Edited by
Peter Roberts, *University of Canterbury, New Zealand*

This series is devoted to cutting-edge scholarship in educational philosophy and theory. Each book in the series focuses on a key theme or thinker and includes essays from a range of contributors. To be published in the series, a book will normally have first appeared as a special issue of *Educational Philosophy and Theory*, one of the premier philosophy of education journals in the world. This provides an assurance for readers of the quality of the work and enhances the visibility of the book in the international philosophy of education community. Books in this series combine creativity with rigour and insight. The series is intended to demonstrate the value of diverse theoretical perspectives in educational discourse, and contributors are invited to draw on literature, art and film as well as traditional philosophical sources in their work. Questions of educational policy and practice will also be addressed. The books published in this series will provide key reference points for subsequent theoretical work by other scholars and will play a significant role in advancing philosophy of education as a field of study.

Titles in the series include the following:

Education, Ethics and Existence
Camus and the human condition
Peter Roberts, Andrew Gibbons and Richard Heraud

Shifting Focus
Strangers and strangeness in literature and education
Edited by Peter Roberts

Philosophy in Schools
Edited by Felicity Haynes

New Directions in Educational Leadership Theory
Edited by Scott Eacott and Colin W. Evers

Expertise, Pedagogy and Practice
Edited by David Simpson and David Beckett

Philosophy and Pedagogy of Early Childhood
Edited by Sandy Farquhar and E. Jayne White

The Dilemma of Western Philosophy
Edited by Michael A. Peters and Carl Mika

Educational Philosophy and New French Thought
Edited by David R. Cole and Joff P.N. Bradley

The Dilemma of Western Philosophy

Edited by
Michael A. Peters and Carl Mika

LONDON AND NEW YORK

First published 2018
by Routledge
2 Park Square, Milton Park, Abingdon, Oxon, OX14 4RN, UK

and by Routledge
711 Third Avenue, New York, NY 10017, USA

Routledge is an imprint of the Taylor & Francis Group, an informa business

© 2018 Philosophy of Education Society of Australasia

All rights reserved. No part of this book may be reprinted or reproduced or utilised in any form or by any electronic, mechanical, or other means, now known or hereafter invented, including photocopying and recording, or in any information storage or retrieval system, without permission in writing from the publishers.

Trademark notice: Product or corporate names may be trademarks or registered trademarks, and are used only for identification and explanation without intent to infringe.

British Library Cataloguing in Publication Data
A catalogue record for this book is available from the British Library

ISBN 13: 978-1-138-08061-4

Typeset in Plantin
by diacriTech, Chennai

Publisher's Note
The publisher accepts responsibility for any inconsistencies that may have arisen during the conversion of this book from journal articles to book chapters, namely the possible inclusion of journal terminology.

Disclaimer
Every effort has been made to contact copyright holders for their permission to reprint material in this book. The publishers would be grateful to hear from any copyright holder who is not here acknowledged and will undertake to rectify any errors or omissions in future editions of this book.

Contents

Citation Information   vii
Notes on Contributors   ix

Introduction: Blind, or Keenly Self-regarding?
The dilemma of Western philosophy   1
Carl Mika and Michael Peters

1 The Humanist Bias in Western Philosophy and Education   4
   Michael A. Peters

2 Counter-Colonial and Philosophical Claims: An indigenous
   observation of Western philosophy   12
   Carl Mika

3 Through the Crucible of Pain and Suffering: African-American philosophy
   as a gift and the countering of the western philosophical metanarrative   19
   George Yancy

4 How Can We Overcome the Dichotomy that Western Culture has
   Created Between the Concepts of Independence and Dependence?   36
   Zehavit Gross

5 Rethinking the 'Western Tradition'   42
   Penny Enslin and Kai Horsthemke

6 How the West Was One: The Western as individualist, the
   African as communitarian   51
   Thaddeus Metz

7 Human Freedom and the Philosophical Attitude   61
   Sharon Rider

CONTENTS

8 Doubt, Despair and Hope in Western Thought: Unamuno and
   the promise of education   74
   Peter Roberts

9 The Offerings of Fringe Figures and Migrants   87
   A.-Chr. Engels-Schwarzpaul

10 Actual Minds of Two Halves: Measurement, Metaphor and the Message 103
   Georgina Stewart

11 On the (Im)potentiality of an African Philosophy of Education
   to Disrupt Inhumanity   110
   Yusef Waghid

   Index   117

Citation Information

The chapters in this book were originally published in *Educational Philosophy and Theory*, volume 47, issue 11 (October 2015). When citing this material, please use the original page numbering for each article, as follows:

Introduction
Blind, or Keenly Self-regarding? The dilemma of Western philosophy
Carl Mika and Michael Peters
Educational Philosophy and Theory, volume 47, issue 11 (October 2015)
pp. 1125–1127

Chapter 1
The Humanist Bias in Western Philosophy and Education
Michael A. Peters
Educational Philosophy and Theory, volume 47, issue 11 (October 2015)
pp. 1128–1135

Chapter 2
Counter-Colonial and Philosophical Claims: An indigenous observation of Western philosophy
Carl Mika
Educational Philosophy and Theory, volume 47, issue 11 (October 2015)
pp. 1136–1142

Chapter 3
Through the Crucible of Pain and Suffering: African-American philosophy as a gift and the countering of the western philosophical metanarrative
George Yancy
Educational Philosophy and Theory, volume 47, issue 11 (October 2015)
pp. 1143–1159

Chapter 4
How Can We Overcome the Dichotomy that Western Culture has Created Between the Concepts of Independence and Dependence?
Zehavit Gross
Educational Philosophy and Theory, volume 47, issue 11 (October 2015)
pp. 1160–1165

CITATION INFORMATION

Chapter 5
Rethinking the 'Western Tradition'
Penny Enslin and Kai Horsthemke
Educational Philosophy and Theory, volume 47, issue 11 (October 2015)
pp. 1166–1174

Chapter 6
How the West Was One: The Western as individualist, the African as communitarian
Thaddeus Metz
Educational Philosophy and Theory, volume 47, issue 11 (October 2015)
pp. 1175–1184

Chapter 7
Human Freedom and the Philosophical Attitude
Sharon Rider
Educational Philosophy and Theory, volume 47, issue 11 (October 2015)
pp. 1185–1197

Chapter 8
Doubt, Despair and Hope in Western Thought: Unamuno and the promise of education
Peter Roberts
Educational Philosophy and Theory, volume 47, issue 11 (October 2015)
pp. 1198–1210

Chapter 9
The Offerings of Fringe Figures and Migrants
A.-Chr. Engels-Schwarzpaul
Educational Philosophy and Theory, volume 47, issue 11 (October 2015)
pp. 1211–1226

Chapter 10
Actual Minds of Two Halves: Measurement, Metaphor and the Message
Georgina Stewart
Educational Philosophy and Theory, volume 47, issue 11 (October 2015)
pp. 1227–1233

Chapter 11
On the (Im)potentiality of an African Philosophy of Education to Disrupt Inhumanity
Yusef Waghid
Educational Philosophy and Theory, volume 47, issue 11 (October 2015)
pp. 1234–1240

For any permission-related enquiries please visit:
http://www.tandfonline.com/page/help/permissions

Notes on Contributors

A.-Chr. (Tina) Engels-Schwarzpaul is Associate Professor in Spatial Design at the School of Art and Design, AUT University, New Zealand.

Penny Enslin is Chair of Education at the University of Glasgow, and Professor Emeritus in the School of Education at the University of the Witwatersrand, South Africa.

Zehavit Gross is an associate professor, head of the graduate program of Management and Development in Informal Education Systems in the School of Education and has been appointed to the UNESCO/Burg Chair in Education for Human Values, Tolerance and Peace, Bar-Ilan University, Israel.

Kai Horsthemke is Associate Professor in the Wits School of Education at the University of the Witwatersrand, South Africa, and Fellow at the Oxford Centre for Animal Ethics, UK.

Thaddeus Metz is a distinguished research professor of Philosophy at the University of Johannesburg, South Africa.

Carl Mika is a senior lecturer in the Faculty of Education at University of Waikato, New Zealand.

Michael A. Peters is Professor of Education at the University of Waikato, New Zealand. He is the Executive Editor of *Educational Philosophy and Theory*.

Sharon Rider is Professor of Philosophy at Uppsala University, Sweden, where she served as vice-dean of the Faculty of Arts from 2008 to 2014.

Peter Roberts is Professor of Education at the University of Canterbury, New Zealand.

Georgina Stewart works in the Faculty of Education of the University of Auckland, based at the Tai Tokerau Campus in Whangarei, New Zealand.

Yusef Waghid is Distinguished Professor of Philosophy of Education at Stellenbosch University, South Africa.

George Yancy is Professor of Philosophy at Duquesne University, USA.

INTRODUCTION

Blind, or Keenly Self-regarding? The dilemma of Western philosophy

In 2013, a range of scholars was approached, with a theme and a major question for a special issue of *Educational Philosophy and Theory*. The question was stated in the following way:

- Does the Western tradition have the intellectual resources to overcome its philosophical blindness?

And in a subset the following was also asked:

- Can it [Western philosophy] learn from, by, despite, itself? What are its major resources for this kind of learning? Does it have the capacity to learn from other traditions?

As a special invitation, this was sent out to scholars across the disciplines in the humanities and social sciences to write an invitational short paper in response to this issue. But the questions themselves exposed us to possible accusations of oversimplifying a set of complex problems. This oversimplification can occur in philosophy generally. Often, philosophical traditions are described as if they are geometrical, with one beginning at one point, and another—often its antithesis—taking over somewhere else. These discussions appear overly simplistic and symmetrical, and to evolve as if metaphilosophical discourses in those instances really do adequately represent what they purport to. The most well known of these spatially bound descriptions, at least in Western philosophy, occurs around Continental and analytical philosophy, the gulf between them possibly having its origin in the schism between poetry and philosophy but finding its voice in the famous Carnap/Heidegger disagreement. Each camp has been known to fight for its territory on the basis that it has some province that is its own and has adopted a 'manifesto [that] can be set up like a battlefield' (Caws, 2001). Underlying these positions is the most fundamental pursuit of clarity: identifiably crisp borders between the 'I' and 'you'.

If the battle lines that are drawn between Continental and analytic philosophy appear to be formidable and complex, then our readers may need to be warned that the contributors to this current issue are delivering various assaults of an even more difficult and multifaceted nature. The writers are not just thinking about Western philosophy as a rubric but also, at times, as a phenomenon that needs to be brought into question, with some tentativeness retained about its boundaries. Interestingly, this issue deals with Western philosophical blindness, and some of the contributors' discussions turn on disputing just how clearly demarcable Western philosophy itself really is. In general, the writers hint at its overlap into other traditions. They generally do not want to render too visible that which itself may be, by its nature, incapable of clearly perceiving other philosophical traditions. For the contributors, in some measure or other, the 'I', the Western creator of a manifesto of sheer truth has firmly brought the 'you' over into its philosophical kingdom. It has not just existed neutrally: it has acted against other possibilities, diminishing them but also reconstructing them in new ways. It has thus become a part of other philosophies.

Bringing something as Herculean as Western philosophy to account is no mean feat, and a dominant response centres on its indistinct edges. Even in its own right, as Enslin and Horsthemke propose and as we have seen in the disagreement between Carnap and Heidegger, Western philosophy is diverse. Enslin and Horsthemke argue for a rethink of the 'Western' rubric, itself a transformative and liberating act. Yet thankfully there is a general consensus that one may indeed talk of Western philosophy even if it is now shared by other traditions of thought and even if called such for the sake of convenience. The collection of papers in this issue hence gives us permission to move on from thinking about whether there 'really is' such a thing as Western philosophy and to start considering its texture in different ways. Rider argues this move most clearly by showing that one talks of the characteristics of Western philosophy in order to show its distinctiveness. There is a certain pragmatism referred to here that encourages us to not become bogged down in the problem of whether Western philosophy can or should even be addressed. Moreover, for Rider, there is an ethical need to question anew how Western thought must change, even if these enquiries provoke discomfort. Metz depicts the use of such terms as 'Western' as not necessarily essentialising but as limiting and suggests that the West must become less 'Western' in the narrow sense and question and redefine its scope from its current individualism. For the writers, there certainly is a phenomenon that, in the fashion of Barad, needs to be cut out and defined just momentarily as a *'local* resolution *within* ... inherent ontological indeterminacy'* (Barad, 2003, pp. 801–831). In the context of this issue, this temporary encapsulation must occur, it seems, so that we do not fall victim to any perceived grandiosity (and hence unassailability) of Western philosophy.

So how can the blindness of Western philosophy and its potential to transform itself from that state, be described? There is a common suspicion evident in the contributions of the grand Western narrative. Peters reiterates both Heidegger's and Derrida's respective positions on this problem, reminding us that Western philosophy cannot get to its own ontology through its rational method. It is barred, as it were, from looking at itself. For Peters, the metaphysics of presence is responsible here. One cannot, though, escape metaphysics but instead destabilise it, in the manner of Derrida, so that the absent is brought to the fore. Other philosophical systems, especially African and other indigenous, are considered to be more distant from pure Western thought than others, in particular because they do not have as their core worldview that same origin. Mika argues that indigenous cultures did not traditionally valorise the thoroughgoing rationalism that Western philosophy aspires to, and that if Western thought were more honest it would acknowledge, through its own subjugated philosophies at its disposal, the jolt of mystery that began each seemingly rational perception. Relatedly, Stewart disdains the West's preoccupation with precision through left brain thinking and its subsequent alienation of Maori students in science, arguing instead for a continued exploration of the differences (and an acknowledgement of that continuity) between both hemispheres of thought. Gross proposes that the aim of education is to inculcate a desire to ask where 'thou art' in relation to one's indwelling power. This process of enquiry is distinct from the Western one, which does not set out to ask whether, but merely assumes that the self is separate from other things.

Yancy notes that Western philosophical does not focus comfortably on issues such as race and that its superior idea of itself through its inherited whiteness limits its sight. It is through African American philosophy as what he terms a 'gift' of occasional discomfort that the West can, somewhat ironically, come to see its blindness. It is a phenomenon that troubles the Western self: for Engels-Schwarzpaul, this disturbance comes to the fore in the rifts that occur between supervisor and non-Western student and that open onto the unknown. This lack of certainty in the dynamics between them is potentially transformative for the academy. More broadly but in a similar vein, Roberts argues for an embrace of doubt within education. It is through 'educational agnosticism' that one can encompass doubt and mystery as productive agents.

Quite clearly, Western philosophy is not separate from violence: philosophy is not merely a neutral entity awaiting academic contemplation. Indeed, philosophy may be antidotal to violence, as Waghid proposes it should be. Waghid discusses the African notion of 'ubuntu', an ethics of 'caring and compassionate mutuality', of the disruption to atrocity that comes to being as an unconscious act. On the fact of the relationship between philosophy and resolution, many non-Western and Western philosophers alike would agree, and they may perhaps even state that Western thought—thus demarcated and defined if even just for a fleeting discussion—has consequences bigger than those assumed in mere intellectual discussion. For the current writers in some measure or other, Western philosophy must cease staring into the mirror of its own making, assuming who is fairest of them all. It may be that its own peripheral resources, or those of others, can force the West out of its reverie by drawing its gaze away from its own reflection.

References

Barad, K. (2003). Posthumanist performativity: Toward an understanding of how matter comes to matter. *Signs: Journal of Women and Culture and Society, 28,* 801–831.

Caws, M. (Ed.). (2001). *Manifesto: A century of isms.* Lincoln, NE: University of Nebraska Press.

CARL MIKA
Department of Policy, Cultural, and Social Studies, Faculty of Education
University of Waikato, New Zealand

MICHAEL PETERS
Wilf Malcolm Institute of Educational Research Centre for Global Studies in Education Policy
Cultural and Social Studies in Education, University of Waikato, New Zealand

The Humanist Bias in Western Philosophy and Education

MICHAEL A. PETERS

Wilf Malcolm Institute of Educational Research, University of Waikato

Abstract

This paper argues that the bias in Western philosophy is tied to its humanist ideology that pictures itself as central to the natural history of humanity and is historically linked to the emergence of humanism as pedagogy.

Justine E. Smith (2012) begins an opinion piece for *The New York Times* by posing a question about "Philosophy's Western Bias"

> There is much talk in academic philosophy about the need to open up the discipline to so-called non-Western traditions and perspectives, both through changes to the curriculum and also within the demographics of philosophy departments themselves. These two aspects are seen as connected: it is thought that greater representation of non-Western philosophy will help to bring about greater diversity among the women and men who make up the philosophical community.[1]

But despite intentions, the efforts at achieving a kind of diversity that reflects the contemporary globe and its different philosophical traditions have been a 'tremendous failure'. Smith believes it has failed for two reasons; first, 'non-Western philosophy is typically represented in philosophy curricula in a merely token way' and is not 'not approached on its own terms'; second, 'non-Western philosophy, when it does appear in curricula, is treated in a methodologically and philosophically unsound way' in part because 'it is crudely supposed to be wholly indigenous to the cultures that produce it'. Thus, 'non-Western philosophy remains fundamentally "other"'.

The fact is that 'non-Western philosophy' while crudely reductive, geographically, and historically selective, is also an exclusive Western category itself that normally means the classical philosophies of ancient civilizations, generally Indian, Chinese, and Arabic, crowding out other possible contenders including African philosophies and also indigenous philosophies. Smith draws attention to the ruses that puffs up Western philosophy—the so-called Greek miracle that establishes lineage but is really 'only a historiographical artifact', the inflation of 'West' that really only means specific parts of Europe and its American extension, roughly the size and diversity of the Indian subcontinent.

Smith is right to make these arguments and to question the way that even scholars like Derrida wants to argue for the exceptional place of the Western tradition as the proper home of philosophy and 'humanity' as a whole, a pint that I take up below. He further extends his critique of the Eurocentrism of Western philosophy by criticizing its a historical outlook and 'presentism', writing:

> This stems from the fact that philosophy, modeling itself after the sciences, believes it is closer to the truth than it was in the past, and that if a theory is not true there is little reason to spend much time on it.

Not only does Western philosophy picture itself as attached to truth in a privileged way but also sees itself as autonomous from culture. Somehow it imagines itself to be free of its own cultural embodiment, preferences, and attachments and able to attain a perspective free from its own cultural institutions. This is a critical point and one that reminds me of the serious attempt made by Wittgenstein in his discussions of what is involved in understanding other cultures without collapsing into cultural relativism.[2] In his view, the shared forms of life anchored in humanity's natural history enable us to overcome conceptual differences and epistemic barriers in coming to understand another culture (Saari, 2005). Part of this natural history is that we are language using animals and language 'conditions our nature, conditions our understanding of the world and of ourselves.' As Hacker (2001) explains:

> The humanistic disciplines investigate mankind as cultural, social and historical beings. But we are such beings only in so far as we are also language users. Our animal nature is transformed by our acquisition of, and participation in the cultural institution of, a language.[3]

Wittgenstein's philosophy of language shows 'why the subject matter of the humanistic studies is not in general amenable to the forms of explanation of the natural sciences and why the forms of explanation characteristic of the humanities are different in kind from and irreducible to that of the natural sciences' (Hacker, n.p.). Wittgenstein also shows that a language being a public, rule-governed practice that is constitutive of the form of life and culture of its speakers, 'is essentially shareable by creatures of a like constitution'. Thus, 'Human languages are shared by members of human linguistic communities'.

In a truly global perspective, the Western view is difficult to maintain even if we insist on the so-called autonomy of meaning. Philosophy, unlike science, in the global sense is very much still captured by culture and therefore part and parcel of the business of national identity construction. It is so in most parts of the world, as it is also in the West even if 'we' still insist on philosophy's independence from culture. Referring briefly to Leibniz's reflection that philosophy 'always piggybacks on the commerce of goods' Smith argues:

> Europe becomes the principle locus of philosophical and scientific activity only when it comes to dominate the global economy through the conquest of the New World and the consequent shifting of the economic center of the world from Asia to Europe.

He points the global center is shifting again and with it we must expect a change in philosophy and, perhaps, also in Western philosophy's own self-image. In this new geopolitical reality, Western academic philosophy risks becoming a parochial tradition and he recommends an alternative approach to the history of philosophy that treats 'both Western and non-Western philosophy as the regional inflections of a global phenomenon'.

Smith's arguments have even more force when applied to contemporary Western philosophy of education, especially the now-dominant ethical form that might be roughly described as liberal humanism springing from various historical sources. In an important sense, 'humanism' or 'liberal humanism' is often seen as the heart of the Western tradition going back to Plato and receiving different interpretations in successive ages: classical humanism, Renaissance humanism, Enlightenment humanism, liberal humanism. Humanism harbors the deep and sometimes hidden meaning of Western philosophy's understanding of what is characteristic of or common to human beings. It is also a form of pedagogy rather than a coherent philosophy and for good reason for from the classical beginnings *humanus* had specific meanings linking concepts of 'benevolent' and 'learned' (though this meaning was lost in antiquity and does not form part of the middle Latin or modern derivatives of the term).

Kristeller (1961, p. 9) remarks 'I have been unable to discover in the humanist literature any common philosophical doctrine, except a belief in the value of man and the humanities, and in the revival of ancient learning'. He clarifies that Renaissance humanism is a revival of ancient learning rather than a substantive, coherent, or consistent philosophy. Mann (1996, p. 1) in *The Origins of Humanism* suggests that the term *'umanista* was used, in fifteenth century Italian academic jargon to describe a teacher or student of classical literature including that of rhetoric' and the term only surfaces in the English context nearly a hundred years later to consolidate its meaning as 'humanism' in the nineteenth century.

> The English equivalent 'humanist' makes its appearance in the late sixteenth century with a similar meaning. Only in the nineteenth century, however, and probably for the first time in Germany in 1809, is the attribute transformed into a substantive: *humanism*, standing for devotion to the literature of ancient Greece and Rome, and the humane values that may be derived from them. (p. 2)

Giustiniani (1985, p. 167) provides a clear picture of the meanings of 'humanism':

> 'Humanism' comes from *humanus* which comes from *homo*...[Yet] Human nature is complex and contains conflicting tendencies, and cannot be defined completely or from a single point of view.

THE DILEMMA OF WESTERN PHILOSOPHY

Giustiniani (1985, p. 172) details how the German-speaking world the term 'Humanist' takes on different meanings while retaining its specific meaning as scholar of Classical literature and later

> gave birth to further derivatives, such as *humanistisch* for those schools which later were to be called *humanistische Gymnasien*, with Latin and Greek as the main subjects of teaching (1784). Finally, *Humanismus* was introduced to denote 'classical education in general' (1808) and still later for the epoch and the achievements of the Italian humanists of the fifteenth century (1841). This is to say that 'humanism' for 'classical learning' appeared first in Germany, where it was once and for all sanctioned in this meaning by Georg Voigt (1859).

The bias in Western philosophy is, therefore, intimately linked with the historical emergence of humanism as a form of pedagogy and especially with the revival of the *studia humanitatis* that included *grammatica*, *rhetorica*, poetics, *historia*, and *philosophia moralis*. Kristeller (1990, p. 113) makes clear throughout the Renaissance humanism included the humanities and failed to include 'theology, jurisprudence, and medicine, and the philosophical disciplines other than ethics, such as logic, natural philosophy, and metaphysics'.

The bias of Western philosophy and education is historically deep structuring our understandings in different eras from the Renaissance to the Enlightenment. It was not until the twentieth century that this humanist bias was fully explored as ideological in relation to associated concepts of 'human nature', 'man', and more recently 'humanity'. It was Heidegger (1946) in 'Letter on Humanism'[4] that argued that humanism and the associated concepts should be rejected as metaphysical. Heidegger's 'Letter' was written in response to Jean Beaufret's questions that referenced Sartre's 'Existential is a humanism', an address given a year earlier. Heidegger referred to humanism as a metaphysics that ascribes a universal essence to mankind privileging it above all other forms of existence but ultimately leading to a false subjectivism and idealism.[5] The orientation of human beings, for Heidegger is not to itself but rather beyond itself that he regards as an open possibility.

Louis Althusser taking up Heidegger's famously coined the notion of 'antihumanism' arguing that there is no essence just historical processes. For Althusser, humanism is a form of false consciousness. Structural analysis—of a scientific Marx—can reveal that we are the product of external forces outside the reach of individual rational scrutiny. Many following Althusser's leads end up by criticizing humanism on the basis of its commitments to individuality and to individual rationality. Other critiques have based their criticisms on sexism, racism, and classism. More recently, the critique from ecology has made is mark: a crude anthropological humanism is seen as responsible for a world view that emphasizes humankind at the center of the earth's living systems. Cosmological physics makes a similar kind of argument about the place of humanity in the cosmos only to describe Earth as one planet among one hundred billion star systems.

'Deconstruction,' the term most famously associated with Derrida, is a practice of reading and writing, a mode of analysis and criticism that depends deeply upon an interpretation of the question of style.⁶ In this, Derrida follows a Nietzschean–Heideggerian line of thought that repudiates Platonism as the source of all metaphysics in the West from St Paul to Kant, Mill, and Marx. Where Heidegger still sees in Nietzsche the last strands of an inverted Platonism, tied to the metaphysics of the will to power, and pictures himself as the first genuinely post-metaphysical thinker, Derrida, in his turn, while acknowledging his debt, detects in Heidegger's notion of being a residual and nostalgic vestige of metaphysics. He agrees with Heidegger that the most important philosophical task is to break free from the 'logocentrism' of Western philosophy—the self-presence, immediacy, and univocity—that clouds our view and manifests its nihilistic impulses in Western culture. And yet 'breaking free' does not mean overcoming metaphysics. Deconstruction substitutes a critical practice focused upon texts for the ineffable or the inexpressible. It does so, not by trying to escape the metaphysical character of language but by exposing and undermining it: by fixing upon accidental features of the text to subvert its essential message and by playing off its rhetorical elements against its grammatical structure. Heidegger's strategy for getting beyond 'man' will not do the trick: Derrida suggests that 'a change of style' is needed, one which will 'speak several languages and produce several texts at once', as he says in an early essay, 'The Ends of Man' (Derrida, 1982).

Derrida's work reflects and engages with the tradition of Western metaphysics going back to Plato promoting an understanding of the critique of *phallogocentrism* as a response to the Western metaphysical tradition. Derrida systematically engages with the Western tradition with a humanity, passion, generosity, and with patient and stunning scholarship. Phallogocentrism, (along with logocentrism and Eurocentrism) refer to the privileging not just of European culture over all others but more deeply to the Western metaphysical tradition that holds to a hierarchy of values sustained by a binary logic that cannot do otherwise than privilege one term over another (reality/appearance, speech/writing, presence/absence, identity/difference, life/death). It is the general economy of an inherited humanism propping up all the ideological remnants of Man in his essence and all of the substitutions played out since Nietzsche that deconstruction seeks to destabilize, unmask, and undermine. Deconstruction, going beyond *Abbau* and *Destruktion*, works to undo 'the metaphysics of presence' which holds that thought and speech (the *logos*) is the privileged center through which all discourse and meaning are derived. *Gott ist tot* (God is dead) is the shorthand that Nietzsche uses to proclaim this deepening of humanism.

The 'madman' in *The Gay Science* pronounces:

> God is dead. God remains dead. And we have killed him. How shall we comfort ourselves, the murderers of all murderers? What was holiest and mightiest of all that the world has yet owned has bled to death under our knives: who will wipe this blood off us? What water is there for us to clean ourselves? What festivals of atonement, what sacred games shall we have to invent? Is not the greatness of this deed too great for us? Must we ourselves not become gods simply to appear worthy of it? (Section 125).

God can no longer act as a source or foundation for moral authority so what now can conceivably anchor the system of values? Nietzsche's observation heralds a new secularism in Europe and the end of the effective history of the Church. At least, this is how Heidegger interprets it. The proposition 'God is dead' as he says 'has nothing to do with the assertion of an ordinary atheism. It means: The supersensible world, more especially the world of the Christian God, has lost its effective force in history' (Heidegger, 1985, p. 485). What would it mean to talk of Europe without God, or that the Christian God had become unbelievable, especially after the experiences of the WWI and WWII? On what could a replacement code be based? Moral law derivable from our own rationality? The beginning of liberal humanism and the turn to subjectivity with Descrates and Kant? A kind of naturalism advocated by Hume, that is, a natural sympathy for others? Or should one give up on the search for foundations altogether and deny that moral codes and beliefs have any objective foundation? Can they only be explained psychologically?

I present Derrida as a *profound* humanist (Peters & Biesta, 2009), who commited to the value of truth and the promise of humanity endeavors in order to steer us away from its easy ideological fabrications that ultimately only supports a very tawdry and temporary cultural image of ourselves in one particular historical period. I present him so because he stands in a tradition not only within both contemporary modern traditions influence by Nietzsche–Heidegger nexus and the immediate French tradition dating from Kojeve's lectures on Hegel but also in terms of the immediate inheritance from Sartre and his associates as well as Levinas, Blanchot, Althusser, and his many contemporaries including Deleuze, Lyotard, Kofmann, and Foucault.

Clearly, one has to say also the modern tradition from Descartes and Kant, and, indeed, the tradition all the way back to Plato. I do not want to suggest a unity or origin of tradition but perhaps sustaining threads of a complex skein and we must then also embrace the Hebraic tradition and various modern literary movements as well as those in the European avant garde. By calling Derrida a *profound* humanist, I mean to indicate that Derrida engages directly and systematically with the question of humanism—what it is to be human and its limits and boundaries in technology and animality—and with its continuance by some means. Thus, a continuance through its encompassing of new extensions and mutations of rights in international law, in democracy to come, in the right to philosophize, in the author/writer/reader, in tasks for the new humanities, in an ethics of the other—of hospitality—in the changed conditions for scholarship and media, in the promise of Europe in providing an alternative vision for world institutions, and the governance of globalization.

In view of the ideological nature of humanism, Derrida has devised ways of overcoming the logocentrism he sees at the heart of the Western tradition through attention to the status of the humanities and the attempt to invent new tasks for the humanities facing globalization. There is no doubt that the humanities need new tasks, and Derrida has sought to provide a programmatic picture. That the humanities must also contextualize itself, escaping its local origins and trajectories, and broaden its account to take in the radical pluralism that exists as part of a new globalism that also recognizes the claims of local autonomy made by first peoples, indigenous peoples, sub-state cultural minorities, international religious movements, youth cultures, gender groups, and all sorts of political associations. Here, the question of self and other looms large, as do questions revolving centrally around notion of ethics and politics. Derrida provides us with the rejuvenation of ancient concepts of friendship, the ethics of hospitality, forgiveness, the gift, the invitation that outlines his account of responsibility to the other.

Notes

1. http://opinionator.blogs.nytimes.com/2012/06/03/philosophys-western-bias/?_php=true&_type =blogs&_r=1&.
2. See particularly Wittgenstein's (1987) *Remarks on Frazer's Golden Bough* and the typescript early 1930s that was a prototype for the *Philosophical Investigations* (but eventually notes that were left out) especially his handwritten remarks about 'metaphysics as a kind of magic', where magic was described as 'deep'—see Zengotita (1989).
3. My references are to the paper (that gives no page references) available at http://info.sjc.ox.ac.uk/scr/hacker/docs/Humanistic%20understanding.pdf.
4. I am refering to Frank A. Capuzzi's translation at http://pacificinstitute.org/pdf/Letter_on_%20Humanism.pdf.
5. See Peters (2001) for my treatment of Heidegger's concept of the human being in the 'Letter on "Humanism"' and Derrida's reading of it in "The Ends of Man" in relation to pedagogy. See also Trifonas and Peters (2004, 2005).
6. This section draws on Peters (2007).

References

Derrida, J. (1982). The ends of man. In *Margins of philosophy* (pp. 3–27). Chicago, IL: University of Chicago Press.
Giustiniani, V. R. (1985). Homo humanus, and the meaning of humanism. *Journal of the History of Ideas, 46*, 175.
Hacker, P. M. S. (2001). Wittgenstein and the autonomy of humanistic understanding. In R. Allen & M. Turvey (Eds.), *Wittgenstein: Theory and the arts* (pp. 39–74). London: Routledge. Retrieved from http://info.sjc.ox.ac.uk/scr/hacker/docs/Humanistic%20understanding.pdf
Heidegger, M. (1946). "Letter on Humanism" published as Brief über den Humanismus, in Wegmarken (1919–58). In W. McNeill (Ed.), *Translated as Pathmarks* (pp. 239–276). Cambridge: Cambridge University Press.
Heidegger, M. (1985). The self-assertion of the German university and the rectorate 1933/34: Facts and thoughts. *Review of Metaphysics, 38*, 467–502.
Kristeller, P. O. (1961). *Renaissance thought: The classic, scholastic, and humanist strains*. New York, NY: Harper and Row.
Kristeller, P. O. (1990). Humanism. In C. B. Schmitt & Q. Skinner (Eds.), *The Cambridge history of renaissance philosophy* (pp. 113–114). Cambridge: Cambridge University Press.
Mann, N. (1996). *The origins of humanism*. Cambridge: Cambridge University Press.
Peters, M. A. (2001). Humanism, Derrida, and the new humanities. In G. Biesta & D. Egea-Kuehne (Eds.), *Derrida and education* (pp. 209–231). London: Routledge.
Peters, M. A. (2007). The humanities in deconstruction: Raising the question of the postcolonial university. *Access, 26*(1), 1–11.

Peters, M. A., & Biesta, H. (2009). *Derrida, politics and pedagogy: Deconstructing the humanities.* New York, NY: Peter Lang.

Saari, H. (2005). Wittgenstein on understanding other cultures. *Grazer Philosophische Studien, 68,* 139–161.

Trifonas, P., & Peters, M. A. (Eds.). (2004). *Derrida, deconstruction and education.* Oxford: Blackwell.

Trifonas, P., & Peters, M. A. (Eds.). (2005). *Deconstructing Derrida: Tasks for the new humanities.* New York, NY: Palgrave.

Wittgenstein, L. (1987). *Remarks on Frazer's golden bough.* London: Humanities Press.

Zengotita, T. (1989). On Wittgenstein's remarks on Frazer's golden bough. *Cultural Anthropology, 4,* 390–398.

Counter-Colonial and Philosophical Claims: An indigenous observation of Western philosophy

CARL MIKA

Faculty of Education, Department of Policy, Culture and Social Studies, University of Waikato

Abstract

Providing an indigenous opinion on anything is a difficult task. To be sure, there is a multitude of possible indigenous responses to dominant Western philosophy. My aim in this paper is to assess dominant analytic Western philosophy in light of the general insistence of most indigenous authors that indigenous metaphysics is holistic, and to make some bold claims about both dominant Western philosophy in line with an indigenous metaphysics of holism. There will, of course, be different ways of expressing holism according to the indigenous group, but most of the literature states, as a most basic concern, that a general indigenous philosophy is concerned with the groundedness (or otherwise) of an individual as an entity related to and indivisible from the rest of the world.[1] *The consequences of any assertion about the holistic nature of metaphysics are vast, including for the interpretation of what is often perceived of as the antithesis: Western philosophy.*

The theme of Western philosophy is not a recurring one in the indigenous canon. The reasons for this are beyond the scope of my paper but I suspect they may comprise the following: the urgency of other problems needing (mainly qualitative) research; relatedly, the irrelevancy of dwelling on Western philosophy; and its overwhelming hostility to indigenous thought. It will sometimes form a platform for discussion in academic indigenous works, but it will hardly ever be outlined in glowing terms, for it cannot be denied that indigenous peoples, generally speaking, have a bleak view of the Western tradition of philosophy. From its tendency since the Scientific Revolution (but more fundamentally since Plato) to obsess itself with knowledge above all else, to its almost unconscious move to oust a pursuit of anything that does not deal in a correspondence version of truth, Western philosophy, more than any other discipline, may exemplify for the indigenous mind the dominant horizon of colonizing thought. Importantly, it also lays bare a particular vulnerability that the West, from the indigenous perspective, suffers from when faced with the unknowable. Other disciplines, such as law, medicine, education and sociology and so on, draw on social and political cladding to protect themselves from, and even obscure, that underlying susceptibility. Philosophy, however, should not have recourse to this cover-up: to the indigenous person, it is the ultimate theater in which the real sway of thought, with no façade or cosmetic, must play out to its truest and most fundamental extent.

My hypothetical here is hardly new: the indigenous approach to philosophy does not lie in assessing the truth of a proposition through logic, but in how the self is located in the world. A general indigenous philosophy may look most essentially at how one is positioned in relation to another. This 'other' is most often nowadays a person but it needn't have been traditionally. The other could have been a mountain or a tree, for instance, and philosophical discussions would have ranged from what allowed a thing to manifest to begin with, how one might best sit in tandem with that self-emergence of the thing, and how one might then represent the autonomous (but interrelated with the self) activity of the thing. Silence was often the best mode of interaction with the other (Smith, 2007). Utterances of knowledge or propositions of truth about things were likely secondary to the sheer initial and primordial perception of a phenomenon.

Western philosophy in its dominant form would undoubtedly suggest that this thought belongs in literature or religious studies. Here we meet one of the most entrenched biases of Western philosophy, comprising as it does the very profound and subconscious rejection of the mere *possibility* that non-analytical thought might belong in the discipline of philosophy. Dominant analytic philosophy and its associated domains are fortified quite staunchly against even the mention of other forms of thinking. For the indigenous thinker, this reaction is an emotional and subjective one, not one based on any particular objectivity that, ironically, this particular kind of philosophy claims. It also, again, uncovers a peculiar underbelly of Western philosophy: that, ultimately, it must revert to an emotional response rather than a thoroughgoing detached one. In this, it is likely no different to indigenous philosophy, which similarly reacts along lines of feeling in the very first instance. The difference lies in the fact that indigenous philosophy is clear that thought must be based from the very outset on one's visceral response to a thing. Western philosophy, when viewed from the indigenous perspective, is thus gripped by the very problem that it is attempting to eradicate. Here I should note that paradoxes themselves are not a concern for indigenous thought generally but the sort that disdains feeling whilst being incapable of leaving it alone may be thought of as an unusual juxtaposition to live with.

One arm of philosophy that is allowed to remain in the realms of dominant philosophy, although even then only begrudgingly and as long as it resides on the outskirts, is metaphysics. It is towards this discipline that many of us indigenous writers tend to gravitate, because it promises to explain the very basis of orientation towards the world. Deloria and Wildcat (2001) note that Western metaphysics must be thought about in any discussions of indigenous metaphysics. Calderon (2008), Cajete (2000), and Little Bear (2000) are other indigenous writers that have found it necessary to discuss Western metaphysics. It is for many of us a *political* as much as an abstract problem. It is therefore directly related to the everyday world and is not, as dominant Western philosophy tends to treat it, a 'study'. Thus, the indigenous person that undertakes empirical research, or attends a court or other judicial setting as a witness, or is compelled to fill out a census form, is informed by metaphysics as far as the indigenous thinker is concerned. As far as much indigenous philosophy is concerned, metaphysics simply must be thought of as an integral, infusing element within the world.

It may be that indigenous peoples and the West mean different things when discussing metaphysics. Adorno (2001) suggests that initial phenomena need to be theorized on in order for metaphysics as a discipline to occur. The significance in metaphysics lies in its laying forth as an object of conception. There is some need, I argue, for this approach in indigenous thought as well, because in a colonized reality it is insufficient to recite traditional ideas without a further theorizing on their significance in a counter-colonial sense (even if that counter-colonialism is not overt in that theory). But there are some downsides. To begin with, the phenomena that are to be theorized on are often entities in indigenous thought. In Maori thought, for instance, they may be both substance and non-thing (Marsden, 2003; Mika, 2012). Yet their reach is current; they cannot always (if ever) be perceived but they are simply 'there'. A danger in theorizing on them is that they are then only valid if they are objects of thought. They are hence only 'there' if they are constructed that way. This shift poses a grave threat to the oft-cited metaphysics of indigenous holism. Another problem lies in what happens to the indigenous person in the process of pure thought: the self moves above those things being considered and they are removed from what Heidegger (1971) terms the Fourfold and Durie (1994) calls the 'whare tapa wha'. To the indigenous observer, Western philosophy's analysis and scientism—its self-sufficiency—is a dangerous outcome of this most primal of comportments.

Similarly, the construction of space and time as sheer modes of perception may not be one that indigenous peoples share with Kant. Perception for indigenous peoples is not a supporting actor to that ultimate winner—conception—but is extremely important on its own (admittedly as it was for Kant). Seen in this light, it is also essential for indigenous peoples to propose something other than Kant's insistence that space and time are merely perceptual templates. Instead space and time are often directly entangled—even indistinguishable from—entities that, as I have noted, are both substantial and nothing. The Maori term for both space and time—wā—is intimately connected with the notion of 'whakapapa', which is often translated as 'genealogy' but, more importantly, indicates how things appear and remain concealed in their own time through 'Papa' ('Earth Mother'). Things perceived are thus permanently imbued with that initial aspect of presence and absence that characterize the Earth Mother. A Maori perception of an object is colored by that continual paradox: The object is intrinsically related to it and even (to continue the paradox) affects that Maori perceiver. It is indeed the ability to perceive the object in this way, I speculate, that may dictate one's wellbeing. If one is permitted to acknowledge the ground of perception—and hence the object—as both ultimately beyond one's cognitive capacity and as a living entity that contains to it thoroughly unknowable and imperceptible characteristics, then one may retain wellness. If, on the other hand, the indigenous self is forced to view the object as merely a product of something originating from the self, and hence an object of thought, then a kind of violence is done as a whole.

Thus far my discussion has centered on the genre of Western philosophy that currently holds sway. It needs to be signaled—for the indigenous thinker as much as the West—that there is a great wealth of potential in the Western tradition that does not belong solely to the dominant method. That there is some striking anti-colonial thinking in some forms of Western philosophy and, moreover, even some propositions that can be drawn on to *thetically* assert aspects of indigenous experience, should be acknowledged by us. But for the West, the need to tap into this hidden but real form of knowledge is even more pressing. Here I allude to aspects of philosophy that have originated from 'the Continent'. Although many Anglo-Americans take up so-called Continental philosophy with some gusto, too often in philosophy departments they remain the minority. The disagreement between Carnap and Heidegger (Friedman, 2000), focusing on Heidegger's position on nothingness, is informally believed to herald the big division between analytic and Continental philosophy, although the schism started with Russell's and Moore's repudiation of Hegelian idealism (Mander, 2013), and the overall, much earlier divide between philosophy and poetry (Barfield, 2011), I suggest, fuelled the distance between these schools of thought. These arguments may explain the dearth of phenomenology and existentialism in many English-speaking philosophy departments and the obvious dominance of other disciplines of thought.

Yet for the indigenous person it is in the Continental disciplines that the West may find some respite from these problems. I am quick to give one significant disclaimer here. Kant, bringing together empiricism and rationalism, and challenging indigenous thought as I have outlined earlier, nevertheless possesses some of the traits of his contemporaries—characteristics which are seen as embodying the more orthodox 'Continental' philosophy. He shares the belief of the Early German Romantics, for instance, that the thing-in-itself cannot be known. Indigenous peoples, if they reflect on that, might come to that conclusion as well. But even then the thing-in-itself cannot remain unaddressed, for it is the continued impact of the thing-in-itself, despite its imperceptibility, that is important for indigeneity. It is in the possibility that the thing cannot be conceived of in its totality, but nevertheless be utterly involved in dictating how one proceeds to represent and talk about it, that is crucial. Here we return again to the atmospheric state of the thing, emerging as it does from an origin that is unknowable but affective. The thing in itself, despite not being cognitively graspable, is still hugely important for the self and the self's orientation towards things in the world.

Kant goes some way in developing a tentative approach to knowing a thing but others manage this feat more radically. Like Kant, the Early German Romantics bring a halt to thoroughgoing rationalism; yet they go further by suggesting that a thing shows itself according to the arrangement of Being/the Absolute. For Novalis, this is also a *political*, not solely a philosophical, issue that humanity must be aware of. He had identified that the colonization of a people brought about metaphysical changes at an extremely profound level. The self-colonization of his community was a high priority for him, and some of its signs comprised the following: the pursuit of numbers to stand in for things (Novalis, 1960b); the idea that Being is centered in the self (he critiqued Fichte for this very belief) (Novalis, 1960c); generally, the dominant proposition that a thing has only cognitive value (and is merely a product of cognition); and the introduction of a static system of writing (Novalis, 1960a). Schelling, Hölderlin, and Schleiermacher were, like Novalis, concerned with the staticising of the world and with the suggestion that humans were somehow thoroughly self-evident. Against that view, they proposed that one had to think of the world in terms of its inherent possibilities: for Novalis, this engaged with a process of lifting a concept of things from the banal to the mysterious, which shares some commonalities with Heidegger's (1977) 'saving power'. Thinking of the potential of entities involved accommodating the problem of not pretending to represent them in full, as to do so has a detrimental impact on the world in some way.

In this process, they also encourage the Western thinker to philosophize *away from* those original thinkers' prescribed sphere. Here I make an extremely bold and possibly very contentious observation: that Western philosophy has become too name-centric, where the great thinkers have become too pivotal to thinking. I speak tentatively here, because other indigenous writers may not share this observation. Yet, there does seem to be a marked difference between the recounting of indigenous and Western philosophy. I speculate that indigenous philosophy, as it appears in the literature, does not draw heavily on particular individuals so vehemently as Western philosophy does. Written indigenous philosophy engages instead more with, and drills deeply into, a fundamental cultural phenomenon—not through the lens of another individual, but with the writer bringing together the spheres of lived experience, intellect, and the unknown. Whilst this difference between the two could just be the result of a cultural nuance, to the indigenous thinker it may also signal a divergence in focus, where dominant (not all) Western scholarship defaults to the prized and comfortable zone of previous thinkers. If my suspicions here are credible, then thought in this vein is barred from entering into the endless possibilities that a thing offers. One just draws on the same paradigm to tell another story.

How then, if at all, can indigenous thought assist Western philosophy to acknowledge its emotional origins and, moreover, to allow for the emotional response to the mystery of a thing? Because indigenous thought has been philosophically and politically so marginalized, these questions are especially confronting. There is a social reality to the consequences of any answer that most indigenous writers will have at the forefront, comprising such problems as the misappropriation of indigenous thought, the inappropriate application of it, the warping of it and so on. Perhaps the first step involves the West resorting to the vast reservoir of its own thought, *through*, but not *totally reliant on*, some of its individuals that insist on a continued recognition of mystery. The emphasis in my suggestion is deliberate, because I want to propose that the continued thinking of mystery—the dual hiddenness and presence of an entity, the relationship of the entity to the self beyond the cognitive, the entity's participation in Being, and so on—may best be carried out with initial recourse to a previous thinker but, most importantly, with a subsequent and wild freedom of thought. At some point, the indigenous community may then wish to engage the West in discussions on how to progress thought that acknowledges the continued 'All', but not before observing how the West deals with its own theoretical source.

Dominant Western philosophy is impressive in its gigantic and immovable enterprise of logic and rational thought, but to the indigenous thinker those aspects that allow it to remain so colossally solid are simultaneously its vulnerability. The solutions to its difficulties lie submerged within other, less central, modes of Western thinking that develop and encourage thought towards an approximation of a thing in all its complexity and its interdependence with all other things, including the self. Those other forms of Western thought are no less impressive. Seen in this light, thinking through the eyes, but also transcending the influence, of the philosophers who are largely overlooked in Western literature, may prove to be a step away from the blindness that Western philosophy manifests for the indigenous onlooker. To the indigenous person, this step is an important and confronting one for the West: it moves towards the dissolution of what has thus far been colossal and promises the dispersion of thought into an ongoing and mysterious relationship with things in the world.

Note

1. See for instance: Deloria and Wildcat (2001), Calderon (2008), and Marsden (1985) for specific discussion on the nature of indigenous relationships with all things.

References

Adorno, T. (2001). *Metaphysics: Concept and problems.* Stanford, CA: Stanford University Press.
Barfield, R. (2011). *The ancient quarrel between philosophy and poetry.* New York, NY: Cambridge University Press.
Cajete, G. (2000). *Native science: Natural laws of interdependence.* Santa Fe, NM: Clear Light Publishers.
Calderon, D. (2008). *Indigenous metaphysics: Challenging Western knowledge organization in social studies curriculum* (Unpublished doctoral dissertation). University of California, Los Angeles.
Deloria, V., & Wildcat, D. (2001). *Power and place: Indian education in America.* Golden, CO: Fulcrum Resources.
Durie, M. (1994). *Whaiora: Māori health development.* Auckland: Oxford University Press.
Friedman, M. (2000). *A parting of the ways: Carnap, Cassirer, and Heidegger.* Peru, IL: Carus Publishing Company.
Heidegger, M. (1971). *Poetry, language, thought.* (A. Hofstadter, Trans.). New York, NY: Perennial Classics.
Heidegger, M. (1977). *The question concerning technology and other essays.* (W. Lovitt, Trans.). New York, NY: Harper.
Little Bear, L. (2000). Jagged worldviews colliding. In M. Battiste (Ed.), *Reclaiming indigenous voice and vision* (pp. 77–85). Vancouver: UBC Press.
Mander, W. (2013). Hegel and British idealism. In L. Herzog (Ed.), *Europe: Currents, crosscurrents and undercurrents* (pp. 165–176). London: Palgrave Macmillan.

Marsden, M. (1985). God, man and universe: A Maori view. In M. King (Ed.), *Te Ao Hurihuri: The world moves on: Aspects of Maoritanga* (pp. 143–164). Auckland: Longman Paul Ltd.

Marsden, M. (2003). *The woven universe: Selected writings of Rev. Māori Marsden*. Otaki: Estate of Rev. Māori Marsden.

Mika, C. (2012). Overcoming being in favour of knowledge: The fixing effect of mātauranga. *Educational Philosophy and Theory, 44*, 1080–1092.

Novalis. (1960a). Die Christenheit oder Europa. In P. Kluckhohn, & R. Samuel (Eds.), *Schriften: Das philosophische Werk II* [Writings: Philosophical works II] (Vol. 3, pp. 497–524). Stuttgart: W. Kohlhammer.

Novalis. (1960b). Heinrich von Ofterdingen [Henry of Ofterdingen]. In P. Kluckhohn, & R. Samuel (Eds.), *Schriften: Das dichterische Werk* [Writings: Poetic works] (Vol. 1, pp. 183–369). Stuttgart: W. Kohlhammer.

Novalis. (1960c). Philosophische Studien der Jahre 1795/96: Fichte-Studien [Philosophical studies of the years 1795/96: Fichte Studies]. In P. Kluckhohn, & R. Samuel (Eds.), *Schriften: Das philosophische Werk I* [Writings: Philosophical works I] (Vol. 2, pp. 29–296). Stuttgart: W. Kohlhammer.

Smith, C. (2007). Cultures of collecting. In M. Bargh (Ed.), *Resistance: An indigenous response to neoliberalism* (pp. 65–74). Wellington: Huia.

Through the Crucible of Pain and Suffering: African-American philosophy as a gift and the countering of the western philosophical metanarrative

GEORGE YANCY
Department of Philosophy, Duquesne University

Abstract

In this article, I argue that African-American philosophy emerges from a socio-existential context where persons of African descent have been faced with the absurd in the form of white racism (This paper is a substantially revised version on an earlier article. See Yancy, G. (2011). African-American Philosophy through the Lens of Socio-Existential Struggle. Philosophy & Social Criticism, Volume 37: 551–574). The concept of struggle, given the above, functions as both descriptive and heuristic vis-à-vis the meaning of African American philosophy. Expanding upon Charles Mills' concept of non-Cartesian sums, I demonstrate the inextricable link between Black lived experience, struggle, and the morphology of meta-philosophical assumptions and philosophical problems specific to African-American philosophy. Because of the philosophical pretensions of white Western philosophy, with it claims to universal truth and objective knowledge, the particularity *of African-American philosophical concerns with questions of embodiment and race is often deemed ersatz or non-philosophical. In this article, I argue that whiteness as the transcendental norm is productive of a form of ignorance endemic to Western philosophical practices that are myopic and hegemonic. Finally, African-American philosophy is theorized as a gift, as a critical counter-narrative that can be deployed to fissure Western philosophy's narcissism.*

The meaning of African-American philosophy is in process, responding to historical contingencies, and constantly engaging in meta-philosophical reflection. In this sense, African-American philosophy is *not* an essence, but a socially engaged project, one that grows out of a larger socio-historical matrix of change. My approach to

African-American philosophy, and the assumptions that inform that approach, as with every hermeneutic framework, both discloses and yet conceals. One always begins an inquiry *in medias res*. There is no hermeneutic perspective from nowhere. Every perspective (etymologically, 'to look') is a partial, *unfinished* look, a beckoning for one to look again. One might argue, along Merleau-Pontyan lines, that there is always the *promise* of more to see. By foregrounding the social and historical *struggle* of Black people,[1] African-American philosophy reconfigures certain perennial assumptions about the nature of philosophy and the philosopher as conceived within the context of mainstream Western (white) philosophy. Theorizing African-American philosophy within the social matrix of anti-Black racism situates philosophical reflective thought within the concrete muck and mire of *raced* embodied existence, thus deconstructing the myth of philosophy and the philosopher as Olympian, beyond the body, beyond race, godlike, otherworldly. Within the context of discussing the preponderance of African-American philosophers who deal with issues in the area of value theory, political, and social philosophy, Robert Birt argues that 'the leisure and liberty to dwell on metaphysical concerns with Olympian composure ... isn't so easy for an outcast and denigrated people' (Yancy, 1998j, p. 351). Bodies that suffer, bodies in pain, lynched bodies, and mutilated bodies constitute the existentially *lived* reality of Black people in America. I argue that it is within the context of such pervasive existential and experiential suffering (Black *Erlebnis*) that African-American philosophy articulates its normative concerns. The philosophical concerns and sensibilities of African-American philosophy are shaped from the *ground up*; they are shaped from the underside of western philosophical hubris. In stream with Cornel West, any really serious philosophy that grapples with life must make sense of what he calls the 'guttural cry' (Yancy, 1998e, p. 38). For my purposes, African-American philosophy is a critical process of rendering that cry, that scream, and that struggle visible and intelligible. In this regard, I would argue that African-American philosophy is a species of *recovering* philosophy, of forcing philosophy to engage issues that mock abstract reflection and theory or *theoros*, which denotes 'spectator.' Abstract spectatorship is a privilege that Black bodies, within a context of anti-Black racism, cannot afford.

Mills (1998) is also cognizant of the 'rage ... of those invisible native sons and daughters who, since nobody knows their name, have to be the men who *cry* "I am!" and women who demand "And ain't I a woman?"' (p. 10). It is existentially and politically incumbent upon Black bodies, because of their historical malediction (discursive construction as 'inferior' and 'evil'), to demand forms of recognition. And yet, it is a form of demand that already asks too much. It is akin to Frederick Douglass's impatience with explaining the barbarity of North American slavery. He writes:

> What! am I to argue that it is wrong to make men brutes, to rob them of their liberty, to work them without wages, to keep them ignorant of their relations to their fellow men, to beat them with sticks, to flay their flesh with the lash, to load their limbs with irons, to hunt them with dogs, to sell them at auction, to sunder their families, to knock out their teeth, to burn their flesh, to starve them into obedience and submission to their masters? Must I argue that a system thus marked with blood and stained with

pollution is wrong? No – I will not. I have better employment for my time and strength than such arguments would imply. (Douglass, 1993, p. 144)

Within the context of the non-recognition of Black humanity, Mills explicitly emphasizes the importance of rage that is expressed by persons of African descent who have been deemed sub-persons/*Untermenschen*. In stream with Mills, I theorize the meaning of African-American philosophy within the context of Black sub-personhood. After all, Black people have had to engage in socio-existential struggle to redefine themselves against longstanding historical racist acts of dehumanization and brutalization. As West (1982) argues, 'The notion that black people are human beings is a relatively new discovery in the modern West' (47). Hence, modernity, with its emphasis upon individualism, advancement, and the critique of traditional beliefs and norms, is undergirded by a form of misanthropy, by fear of the Black body, and by racial markings of the Black body as sub-human, ersatz, primitive, expendable. Hence, one might argue that modernity is parasitic upon the denigration of the Black body, where the meaning of the *anthropos* is grounded upon whiteness. As Frantz Fanon writes,

> That same Europe where they were never done talking of Man, and where they never stopped proclaiming that they were only anxious for the welfare of Man: today we know with what sufferings humanity has paid for every one of their triumphs of the mind. (Fanon, p. 312)

In his genealogical account of modern racism, West provides a narrative that refuses to obfuscate the racial and racist foundations of modernity. He shows 'the way in which the very structure of modern discourse *at its inception* produced forms of rationality, scientificity, and objectivity as well as esthetic and cultural ideals which require the constitution of the idea of white supremacy' (West, 1982, p. 47). Hence, I conceptualize African-American philosophy as a counter-voice to whiteness as a site of hegemonic metanarrative nation building, a site of terror and the desire for totality. In other words, African-American philosophy introduces fissures, differences, and heterogeneity vis-à-vis the white normative *same*. On this score, Jean-Francois Lyotard writes:

> Finally, it must be clear that it is our business not to supply reality but to invent allusions to the conceivable which cannot be presented. And it is not to be expected that this task will effect the last reconciliation between languages games ... only the transcendental illusion ... can hope to totalize them into a real unity. But ... the price to pay for such an illusion is terror. The nineteenth and twentieth centuries have given us as much terror as we can take. We have paid a high price for the nostalgia for the whole and the one, for the reconciliation of the concept and the sensible, of the transparent and the communicable experience ... Let us wage war on totality; let us be witnesses to the unpresentable; let us activate the differences and save the honor of the name. (cited in Gray, 1996, p. 377)

My discussion of African-American philosophy is defined in relationship to its explicitly non-Cartesian or anti-Cartesian assumptions. This is not a novel approach, but it transcends the familial 'Oedipal conflict' subtext that is often associated with so many thinkers who eagerly unseat the patriarch of modern philosophy. To think of the history of Western philosophy as constituting a family with cross generational (*monochromatic*) ties, it is important to note that Black people were never even part of the family; they were always already outsiders, deemed permanently unfit to participate in the normative philosophical community. A non-Cartesian approach to African-American philosophy is conceptually fruitful given the oppression of persons of African descent during European modernity; it is an approach that is prepared to wage war against conceptual totalization. Black people are those who occupy the underside of modernity; they constitute the primitive 'Other' of modernity's self-understanding. Because various Cartesian epistemological assumptions and moves are crucial to modernity, the Cartesian predicament becomes, as (Mills, 1998) demonstrates, 'a kind of pivotal scene for a whole way of doing philosophy and one that involves a whole program of assumptions about the world and (taken-for-granted) normative claims about what is philosophically important' (p. 8). Given the materially and ideologically reinforced sub-personhood status of Black people in North America, what Jean-Paul Sartre calls 'that super-European monstrosity' (Sartre, 26), African-American philosophy is referentially *this*-worldly; it is a site of conceptualizing the world that looks suspiciously upon and rejects the *ahistorical* nature of the epistemic subject. As Crispin Sartwell observes:

> Left to my own devices, I *disappear* as an author. That is the 'whiteness' of my authorship. This whiteness of authorship is, for us, a form of authority; to speak (apparently) from nowhere, for everyone, is empowering, though one wields power here only by becoming lost to oneself. But such an authorship and authority is also pleasurable: it yields the pleasure of self-forgetting or apparent transcendence of the mundane and the particular, and the pleasure of power expressed in the 'comprehension' of a range of materials. (Sartwell, 1998, p. 6)

African-American philosophy's point of critical embarkation is not preoccupied with 'the danger of degeneration into solipsism, the idea of being enclosed in our own possibly unreliable perceptions, the question of whether we can be certain other minds exist, the scenario of brains in a vat, and so forth' (Mills, 1998, p. 8). To get a sense of the non-Cartesian, *this*-worldly constitution of African-American philosophy, consider a few philosophical assumptions held by René Descartes.

In his *Meditations on First Philosophy*, Descartes (1637/1998) assumes the posture of a skeptic. After describing what he depicts metaphorically as having fallen into a whirlpool, a vortex that has tossed him around and thrown him off of his epistemological footing, he reaches his Archimedean point, the indubitable insight that '"I am, I exist" is necessarily true every time I utter it or conceive it in my mind' (sec. 25). Knowing incontrovertibly *that* he exists, Descartes (1637) will shut his eyes, stop up his ears, and withdraw all of his senses in order to uncover the nature of the self. As he says, 'I will attempt to render myself gradually better known and more familiar to myself' (sec. 34). This approach has embedded within it the assumption that the self can be better known through withdrawing from (or radically doubting) the social world, thus challenging the notion that the self is fundamentally socially transversal, constituted dialectically, and thereby inextricably linked to the reality of the social world, its dynamism, and its force of interpellation. Descartes' point of epistemic embarkation is antithetical to Fanon's sociogenic approach to the lived experience of Black people; indeed, Descartes' approach places under erasure precisely the philosophical lens through which Black life can be understood, especially within the context of its lived racist trauma.

The Cartesian approach also presumes that the predicament of the Cartesian self is a universal (de-contextualized) predicament (Mills, 1998, p. 8), one unaffected by the exigencies and contingencies of concrete history. In short, Cartesian epistemic subjects (denuded, as it were, of historical and corporeal *particularity*) are substitutable pure and simple, and faced with the same epistemic global problems, which I see as a species of totalization. This substitutability assumption places under erasure important markers of African-American philosophy, how African-American philosophy, with its questions, problems, and dilemmas, evolves out of a context where *raced* embodied subjects undergo shared existential crises of struggle within the context of anti-Black racism. This does not mean that African-American philosophy does not share philosophical concerns with other philosophical traditions and paradigms, and that there are not points of conceptual cross-fertilization. However, to understand African-American philosophy one must reject the substitutability assumption in favor of a perspective that focuses on and highlights the relationship between social ontology and particular aspects of Black *Erlebnis*, that is, the range of ways in which Black people make meaning within the context of various occurrences or experiences where, in this case, anti-Black racism is salient. In this way, African-American philosophy, with its specific philosophical concerns and articulations, does not aspire to forms of universalism (thus repeating the normative assumptions of whiteness) that obfuscate modes of particularity. Moreover, African-American philosophy does not presume to speak for all epistemic subjects *simpliciter*. Its point of philosophical embarkation does not rest upon the assumption of a fixed set of abstract and universal problems or solutions. Leonard Harris eludes to this view where he argues that 'as a genre, it [African-American philosophy] is dominated by issues of practicality and struggle, which means that it is not committed to a metaphysics in the sense of having a singular proposition out of which all other propositions arise' (Yancy, 1998g, p. 214). And describing his important first anthology, published in 1983, a text which was/is historically pivotal in terms of gathering together important Black philosophical themes and figures, indeed, rendering Black philosophical voices visible, Harris writes, '*Philosophy Born of Struggle* is predicated on the assumption that a good deal of philosophy from the African-American heritage is a function of the history of the struggle to overcome adversity and to create' (Allen, 1991, p. 273). It is important to note that the very publication of Harris's text grew out of struggle. Within a context where 'important' philosophical texts are determined by white consumption and white norms of canon formation, Harris notes, 'There wasn't anybody who was willing to publish it. Not a single publisher in philosophy' (Yancy, 1998g, pp. 218–219). Even Howard University Press, the press of an important HBCU, would not publish Harris' text because of its narrowly defined 'Negro genre' (Yancy, 1998g, p. 219).

THE DILEMMA OF WESTERN PHILOSOPHY

While the complexity of African-American philosophy should not be reduced to struggle, its historical genesis as a professional field of inquiry, its salient themes, and its forms of praxes, presuppose a world of white supremacy, a world that is fundamentally anti-Black. Unlike Descartes, Black self-understanding grows out of a social matrix of pain, suffering, and trauma; a site where the Black body is marked as inferior, different, and deviant. To withdraw from the senses in the style of Descartes, which is a form of negating embodiment as a necessary condition for self-understanding, is to presume an abstract subject from *nowhere*. As such, this move actually renders the self incapable of knowing itself, as self-understanding is always already from a *here*, a place of lived embodied knowledge, a *here* that presupposes a community of intelligibility, the space of sociality. Hence, to understand Black *lived* experience, and to understand African-American philosophy, it is important to begin with embodiment, history, and *lived* social context, a context within which Black people were/are reduced to an epidermal logic that signifies pure externality, thus denying any subjective interiority to the Black body. The Black self, then, is not enclosed within a solipsistic bubble free of interpellation and oppression. The Black self has struggled to understand and define itself within a context where whiteness functions as a transcendental norm, where white embodied others' ego-genesis is parasitic upon the ontological distortion and nullification of Black bodies. Within this context, then, Black bodies *can't afford*, as implied by Sartwell, to engage in the pleasure of self-forgetting or the apparent transcendence of the quotidian and the particular. To forget would result in a form of intellectual masturbation that would seduce Black bodies into a vortex of self-forgetting/self-negation, and thus perpetuate the illusion of white universality or Western philosophical myopia. Hence, whiteness as synonymous with humanity is purchased not only through opposition, but *negation*. As Frantz Fanon argues, 'When I search for Man in the technique and style of Europe, I see only a succession of negations of man, and an avalanche of murders' (Fanon, 321). The Black self is raced and so rendered non-normative [read: not white]. On this score, whiteness is deemed normative and un-raced. As Cone (1986) notes, 'Whites can move beyond particular human beings to the universal human being because they have not experienced the reality of *color*' (p. 86).

To understand Black-being-in-the-world, and the historical context of African-American philosophy, the self-Other dialectic is crucial. Not only is it a fundamental assumption of African-American philosophy, but the self-Other dialectic captures the concrete reality of racism. While racism is not a necessary feature of the self-Other dialectic, the former presupposes the latter. Hence:

1. the self is dynamically plastic;
2. the self does not exist prior to the existence of Others, or, the self is not pre-given or the result of auto-genesis; and
3. The self is always already ensconced within a larger historical context of prejudices and value-laden assumptions that mediate and shape self-understanding and the understanding of the world and Others.

In their effort to delineate various generative themes that give rise to the views of Black philosophers within their text, *I Am Because We Are: Readings in Black*

Philosophy, Hord and Lee (1995) emphasize the self-Other dialectic as one important theme. They argue that 'constitutive of the black philosophical tradition ... is the idea that identity of the individual is never separable from the sociocultural environment. Identity is not some Cartesian abstraction grounded in a solipsistic self-consciousness' (p. 7). The *sum* (I am) of the self is not self-constituted; rather, 'I am' presupposes 'they are.' The Cartesian self, in its isolated self-certainty has no need for the category of sociality; rather, it appears to inhabit a non-social space of invulnerability and independence. African-American philosophy, however, does not begin with an egologically fixed and estranged self; for 'the experience of the self with other selves is the meaning of "sociality"' (Natanson, 1970, p. 47). African-American philosophy begins within a space of profound vulnerability. And while the we-relationship that constitutes any particular self might be taken for granted, the reality of the we-relationship is decisive and its constitutive dynamism precedes the performative 'I am.' As Maurice Natanson (1970) notes, 'We are before I am' (p. 47).

Read through the lens of white racism, the point here is that African-American philosophy presupposes a social ontology where the self, in this case the Black self, is positioned by anti-Black racist forces in terms of which the Black self must contend. In its racially configured form, the self-Other dialectic is captured implicitly by West (1995) where he asks, 'What does it mean to be a philosopher of African descent in the American empire?' (p. 356). West's question raises the issue of philosophical identity beyond the sphere of armchair contemplation and *thinking substances*. His question presupposes an identity in context, a situated self, one that is anti-essentialist in its constitution. Within the American empire, an embodied Black self is always already the target of vicious gazes and acts of brutality. Hence, within the context of racist hegemony, the centrality of the American empire becomes an important axis around which African-American philosophical identity must be defined. Outlaw (1996) even sees the very attempt by Black people to address important meta-philosophical concerns around the issue of whether or not there can be a Black philosophy as an outgrowth of struggle. He notes that confronting 'this issue of "Black philosophy" is the expansion of the continuing history-making struggles of African and African-descended peoples in this country (and elsewhere) to achieve progressively liberated existence as conceived in various ways' (p. 23). Indeed, while African-Americans received PhD's in the field of philosophy prior to the activism and liberating struggles to establish Black Studies Programs in the 1960s and 1970s, it is important to note that the overall raising of consciousness during this period functioned as a catalyst for African-Americans who entered advanced degree programs in the area of philosophy. Hence, in this respect, African-American philosophy is an outgrowth of a larger socio-political struggle of Black people to gain civil rights and human rights. African-American philosophy is therefore an expression of larger processes of epistemic decolonization and epistemic liberation. Yet, these processes also have freeing implications for Western philosophy, especially as it takes itself as *the hub* of universal thought, being, and value. African-American philosophy offers the gift of second-sight which is capable of instilling in Western philosophy, a productive form of white double consciousness. I will return this concept at the end of this essay. The question regarding philosophers of African descent within the context of the American empire bespeaks the role of power and oppression as important foci of African-American philosophical engagement. The philosophical selves that are implicated in West's (1995) question are selves that take seriously 'the worldliness of one's philosophical project' (p. 357). West (2005) also rejects the Cartesian presumption regarding 'the absolute autonomy of philosophy' (p. 8). For West (2005), Cartesians assume that 'philosophy stands outside the various conventions on which people base their social practices and transcends the cultural heritages and political struggles of people' (p. 8). He concludes, 'If the Cartesian viewpoint is the only valid philosophical stance, then the idea of an Afro-American philosophy would be ludicrous' (p. 8). Indeed, any philosophy that takes seriously the importance of struggle against oppression through the exercise of human agency rejects philosophy as a practice that transcends the horror, messiness, and joy of human existence. Within the context of this article, existential struggle not only denotes the historical matrix out of which African-American philosophy evolved/evolves, but the motif of struggle also functions as a source for meta-philosophical insight. Hence, struggle, as used here, is not only descriptive, but heuristic.

Out of his successful effort to teach an introductory course in African-American philosophy for the first time, Mills (1998) shares that he effectively deployed the unifying theme of 'the struggles of people of African descent in the Americas against the different manifestations of white racism' (p. 6) as an important point of critical and insightful inquiry. Mills especially emphasized how Black people were/are defined as sub-persons and how this sub-personhood is an example of what he terms *non*-Cartesian *sums*. Mills' approach helps to flesh out in insightful ways West's point regarding the non-Cartesian sensibilities of African-American philosophy. Mills argues that if we take seriously the conception of sub-personhood, and how such a status presupposes a certain social ontology, then the morphology of philosophical questions asked and which philosophical issues and themes are deemed serious and relevant will be different. He contrasts a Cartesian *sum* with a non-Cartesian *sum* or the kind of *sum* that is portrayed in Ralph Ellison's text, *Invisible Man* (1947). Descartes was pained with questions about solipsism, whether or not he could know with certainty that the external world exists, and whether or not he could distinguish between when he was dreaming as opposed to being awake. These sorts of questions presuppose a range of implicit assumptions about the self, the world, and one's *lived* experiences. Ellison's invisible man, however, does not doubt his existence in the privacy of a stove heated room; rather, he is made to feel invisible, he is made to feel insignificant, within a public anti-Black transactional space where whites refuse to see him, refuse to respect him. The drama of his invisibility takes place *between* selves. Of course, the Black self is not deemed a Thou, but an ontologically truncated self, and in other cases not a self at all. As Descartes *doubts* his own existence, Ellison's invisible man is constantly *reminded* of the denial and diminishment of his self/existence. According to Ellison's (1947) invisible man, 'I am invisible, understand, simply because people (in this case white people) refuse to see me' (p. 3). Lynch mobs make a sham of Cartesian hyperbolic doubt. The vitriol of white racism forces one to be ever cognizant of the existence of other minds, not in vats, but as embodied and raced. Solipsism has no place in a world where Black bodies are mutilated and burned for the pleasure of others. Hence, for Black people, the philosophical problem is not whether one exists or not, but how to collectively resist a white supremacist world of absurdity where one is degraded, marginalized, humiliated, oppressed, and brutalized. On this score, taking flight into the sphere of a private subjectivity is overwhelmed and mocked by the sheer weight of racial violence. Within the context of colonization, Fanon (1963) suggests that this hermetic turn inward is an idol that the colonized will abolish. He writes, 'The colonialist bourgeoisie had hammered into the native's mind the idea of a society of individuals where each person shuts himself up in his own subjectivity, and whose only wealth is individual thought' (p. 47). For Fanon, the very concept of friend within the colonial context belies subjective withdrawal. Friendship presupposes an always already preexisting social matrix and signifies a centrifugal process of mutual recognition. Fanon (1963) notes, 'Brother, sister, friend—these are words outlawed by the colonialist bourgeoisie' (p. 47).

Sociality is the matrix within which racist action takes place. It is within the mundane everyday world that Black people struggle *to be and attempt to make sense of their existence*. Existence in Black, then, which is a fluid site of identity formation and the articulation and re-articulation of meaning within the matrix of sociality, presupposes a set of social ills that are conspicuously absent vis-à-vis an ego that takes itself to exist as an island unto itself. As socially embedded and embodied, existence in Black speaks critically to the narrowness of the field of Western philosophy. To do philosophy in Black within a social context of white racism, where one's very existence is at stake, where one is reduced to a sub-person, even by those white philosophers who have been canonized within the Western philosophical tradition (Hume, Kant, and Hegel, to name a few), one must critically engage and overthrow Western philosophy's misanthropy, its philosophical narcissism. Even Friedrich Nietzsche (1966), though critical of philosophers who 'pose as if they had discovered and reached their real opinions through the self-development of a cold, pure, divinely unconcerned dialectic,' (p. 5) and whose work is held to have critical affinities with African-American thought,[2] argues that Negroes are representative of prehistory and that they are able to endure pain or 'severe internal inflammations that would drive even the best constituted European to distraction' (Nietzsche, 1989, p. 68). Moreover, to do philosophy in Black, one must critique Western philosophy's thanatonic normative assumptions. Indeed, one must be suspicious and critical of *dead* philosophical idols and metaphors, fossilized and existentially inconsequential, that fail to speak to the lives of Black people. Within this context, West (1995) emphasizes the importance of dedisciplinizing modes of knowledge. He writes, 'To dedisciplinize means that you go to wherever you find sources that can help you in constituting your intellectual weaponry' (p. 357). Disrupting the disciplinary 'purity' and marshaling discursive material that speaks to the lives of Black people is what Angela Davis did as early as 1969. When she began to teach philosophy at UCLA, she discovered that 'there was not a single course that had anything to do with African-American ideas' (Yancy, 1998c, p. 23). She decided to design a course where she got students to compare Frederick Douglass's understanding of the slave–master relationship with particular passages in Hegel's *Phenomenology of Spirit*. She notes, 'I found that it was extremely important to legitimate the production of philosophical knowledge in sites that are not normally considered *the* philosophical sites' (Yancy, 1998c, p. 23). In this regard, African-American philosophers engage in legitimization practices that install counter-discursive philosophical sites for doing philosophy. African-American philosophy not only functions as a site of knowledge production, but the production of counter-axiological frames of reference that value alternative spaces where the *love of wisdom* is a community practice.

Drawing from the work of William Barrett, Outlaw (1996) argues that professional philosophy is a site of deformation. This deformation is

> evidenced by the degree to which the 'problems' of philosophy continue to be, even in these very problematic times, discipline immanent, thus without foundation beyond the boundaries of the discipline itself. *They have not emerged from the practices of life.* (p. 25)

The fact that some philosophers of African descent leave 'philosophy' or are unwanted in various philosophy departments is linked to the disciplinary hegemony, philosophical narrowness, and racist practices of so many Anglo-American departments of philosophy. Not only does Lewis Gordon point out that he was denied a position in a philosophy department because it was said that he might attract "too many Black people" (Yancy, 1998h, p. 112), but he argues that even those Black philosophers who primarily do logic and epistemology are at risk of not being hired by particular philosophy departments if they also raise serious questions about what it means to live in a racist culture as Black people, that is, questions that counter the legitimating practices of mainstream philosophy. Gordon argues that if the universities found this out 'then that person is automatically not going to be considered at that institution in the department of philosophy' (Yancy, 1998h, p. 112). Commenting on the need to have African-American philosophers well-placed in departments of philosophy, Laurence Thomas notes, 'I believe that no philosophy department in America would hire a Black who would trouble the waters' (Yancy, 1998f, p. 293). And, yet, African-American philosophy is itself a site of *parrhesia* or courageous speech as it dares to trouble the waters of Western philosophy's tendency to create racist mythopoetic constructions of its own self-image. What becomes obvious is that philosophy's disciplinary bias and its prevalent monochromatic exclusive membership have militated against the presence of Black people. Harris describes the case of Broadus N. Butler, who received his PhD in philosophy as early as 1952 from the University of Michigan, to illustrate an important point about racism and the profession. After he received his doctorate, Butler applied to teach in a mostly white university. According to Harris (1983), Butler found out that his letter of reference stated, '"a good philosopher, but of course, a Negro," and the one-line response, "Why don't you go where you will be among your own kind?"' (p. ix). Like contemporary White-topias, Black philosophers are marked as unwanted and assigned to the back of the proverbial philosophical bus.

Gordon insists upon 'raising the question of whether philosophy has been responsible to itself in terms if what it is' (Yancy, 1998h, p. 112). Raising the important issues of intersectionality, Anita Allen asks, 'With all due respect, what does philosophy have to offer to Black women? It's not obvious to me that philosophy has anything special to offer Black women today' (Yancy, 1998d, p. 172). Given this, what becomes especially relevant is West's observation that 'a relativizing of the discipline's traditional hierarchies of importance and centrality thus becomes necessary' (Mills, 1998, p. 10).

THE DILEMMA OF WESTERN PHILOSOPHY

The logic and significance of West's observation is captured in an example provided by Allen where she talks about studying analytic metaphysics at the University of Michigan. She notes:

> Yet as a Black person it felt odd to sit around asking such questions like 'How do you know when two nonexistent objects are the same?' There you are in the middle of the era of affirmative action, civil rights, women's movements, etc., and you're sitting around thinking about nonexistent objects and how to tell when they are the same. (Yancy, 1998d, p. 168)

Albert Mosley also experienced this tension after he was invited by prominent philosopher of science Rom Harre to study with him at Oxford. Mosley was passionate about conceptual problems in the philosophy of science. Important among these were incommensurability, scientific realism, and the differential accounts of science given by Thomas S. Kuhn and Karl Popper. Mosley applied for a Fulbright and received it. 'But' as he says, '1966–1967 found me torn again between scholarship and activism. I almost refused the Fulbright scholarship because I felt guilty that I was not actively involved in the civil rights struggle' (Yancy, 1998b, pp. 145–155). And while Bernard Boxill was steeped in Bertrand Russell and Alfred North Whitehead's *Principia Mathematica*, and works by Alonzo Church and W. V. O. Quine, he was passionately attracted to all of the discussions and political upheavals around 1965. Boxill eventually wrote his dissertation on the Black Power debate through the lens of Frantz Fanon's work. It is important to note, though, that Boxill did not abandon the tools of analytic philosophy; rather, conceptual analysis was used to address significant issues such as social justice and affirmation action vis-à-vis the lives of Black people.

The insights of Mills, West, Outlaw, Davis, Gordon, Allen, Mosley, and Boxill raise the issue of critically rethinking and transgressing the narrowness of philosophy's self-image. Concerning the paucity of Black people in the field of philosophy, West maintains that philosophy has not been made attractive enough. The image of the philosopher that we have is 'the analytic philosopher who is clever, who is sharp, who is good at drawing distinctions, but who doesn't really relate it to history, struggle, engagement with suffering, how we cope with suffering, how we overcome social misery, etc.' (Yancy, 1998e, p. 38). African-American philosophy's point of embarkation, then, will begin with a different set of existential problematics. W. E. B. Du Bois (1903) points out that, for whites, Black people do not simply have problems; rather, they are a problem people, ontologically so. The very wish 'to make it possible for a man to be both a Negro and an American, without being cursed and spit upon by his fellows, without having the doors of Opportunity closed roughly in his face' (pp. 45–46) already raises significant issues around the struggle for self-definition, political power, and survival. The existential weight of this struggle, which, again, speaks to the reality and importance of sociality, presupposes the capacity of whites who have the political and material power to make non-whites suffer. When one shouts a greeting to the world and the white world slashes away that joy, and one is told 'to stay within bounds, to go back where [you] belong' (Fanon, 1967, p. 115), one must begin with opposition; one must take a stand, one must rethink and critically evaluate one's status within the polity, one must engage in forms of critical thought that enable one best to navigate the terrain of anti-Black racism. Indeed, one must take to task the hidden philosophical anthropological assumptions upon which the polity was/is founded. One must raise the question of philosophy's duty to *this* world, the world of the 'cave,' where white ghostly appearances have killed and brutalized Black bodies in the night. Situated Black bodies within the context of white gazes generate questions regarding the *here* of *embodied subjective* integrity in ways that are more urgent and immediate than traditional Western philosophical discussions regarding the mind-body distinction. Allen notes, 'Two very prominent [white] philosophers offered to look at my resume (I was flattered) and then asked to sleep with me (I was disturbed)' (Yancy, 2008, p. 155).

Allen was reduced to her black body; she became the object of their white sexual fantasies. Here is a context where armchair discussions around the conundrums of the mind-body distinction are transformed into serious matters of ethical and political urgency because of the reality of lived *embodied* distress. Through the white male gaze, *she is her body*. In their eyes, Allen is a 'Jezebel,' the so-called Black slut whose interiority is nullified through the racist mythology that Black women are, as it were, solely constituted as lustful and lascivious. Within the context of white racist mythmaking regarding Black women, Sharpley-Whiting (2005) notes, 'Epitomizing hypersexuality, driven by some racially coded instinct, the black female renders herself available, even assailable, yet simultaneously unassailable, sexually invulnerable, in effect, unrapeable, because of her "licentiousness"' (p. 410). Roberts (1997) argues that in 1736, the South Carolina *Gazette* depicted 'African Ladies' primarily as women who had a 'strong robust constitution,' capable of long sexual endurance, and 'able to serve their lovers "by Night as well as Day"' (p. 11). There is something profoundly hollow about philosophers who sit around leisurely discussing Descartes' bifurcation between two substances (mental and physical) that are deemed really distinct when Black women have been reduced to their bodies and been raped and even lynched, when Black people have been denied *Geist*. Adrian Piper, the first African-American female philosopher to receive tenure, notes:

> I think the primary problem [facing Black women entering the profession of philosophy] is that everybody assumes that Black women are basically maids or prostitutes, and so, you have a lot to get over when you go into a department. (Yancy, 1998a, p. 59)

To be profiled as a prostitute, to be defined as sexually insatiable, to be reduced to one's genitalia, and deemed a prisoner of a presumed 'racial essence,' speaks to the experiential domain of radically non-Cartesian *sums*. Such an experience has no pretensions to a form of de-contextualized universality, where epistemic subjects are substitutable. In fact, such a false universality does an injustice to the intersectional, heterogeneous, *lived* reality of Black women and women of color. Out of the complexity of such experiences grow philosophical assumptions and problems that render philosophical homogeneity deeply suspect. Within this context, for example, issues regarding self-interrogation and the 'nature' of the self do not emerge from a *universal* conundrum. Rather, 'systematic negation of the other person and a furious determination to deny the other person all attributes of humanity' forces Black people to pose constantly: In reality, who am I? (Fanon, 1963, p. 250).

Contra Plato, the practice of African-American philosophy is not one of death, but of life, of affirming life in the face of uncertain non-being. This is not the sort of uncertainty that all of us experience in the face of our inexorable death because of our finitude, where death is the great equalizer. Rather, it is the sort of social death and physical death that Black bodies specifically face in the land of the 'free.' The exclamation, 'Look, a Negro!' has the power to objectify. It has the power, as Fanon (1967) says, to cause 'a hemorrhage that spattered my whole body with black blood' (p. 112). 'A Black man did it!' has ignited forms of racist fanaticism that have resulted in unspeakable forms of bloodlust. Within such a context, the love of wisdom does not delight in immutable truths, but embodies modes of actively engaging in second-order critical reflection toward the end of making sense of one's *situational* and tragic reality and offering engaging critiques of systems of oppression that militate against freedom. From a Black *locus philosophicus*, the love of wisdom (*philo-sophia*) is a form of thought-cum-action. In other words, given the fact of pervasive and systemic anti-Black racism (and how this racism is non-additively linked to issues of class and gender), one way of thinking about African-American philosophy is in terms of a discursive and praxis oriented activity in which philosophers engage in second-order critical reflection on the lived experiences of Black people as they struggle against racist epistemic and normative orders that degrade, dehumanize, and militate against Black self-flourishing. In stream with Herbert Marcuse and Outlaw (1996) in terms of their characterization of critical thought, I would argue that African-American philosophy is a species of *dialectical thought*, a mode of critical engagement that refuses to leave the world unchanged and static in its hubristic and procrustean ways (pp. 29–30). In this regard, African- American philosophy is *negative*; it strives to destabilize the rigid conceptual terrain and normative landscape of Western philosophy's self-constituting and self-perpetuating metanarrative that presupposes whiteness as a given. Yet, understanding Black existence as a site of historically superimposed unfreedom, African-American philosophy deploys its hermeneutic energies toward the *positive* aim of liberation struggle, of securing and asserting *lived* freedom, and telescoping the various ways in which Black people create frameworks of meaning that promote and sustain that freedom. On this score, African-American philosophy inspires existential and socio-political hope and engages in self-validating practices and thereby affirms Black agency and the restructuring of social configurations of power in the quest for equality and the positive advancement of social transformation.[3]

Given the historical facticity out of which African-American philosophy emerges, questions of identity, community, selfhood, respect, dignity, self-determination, resistance, epistemic authority, and psychic survival are philosophically indispensable, they are themes that get configured and reconfigured within the context of a collective journey through the crucible of American racism. Mills (1998) notes, 'African-American philosophy is thus inherently, definitionally *oppositional*, the philosophy produced by property that does not remain silent but insists on speaking and contesting its status' (p. 9). In this way, African-American philosophy asserts a philosophical anthropology that opposes misanthropy and calls into question many of the normative assumptions of modernity—the nature of rationality and who qualifies as human. Against the racist procrustean tendencies of modernity, Blacks have had to engage in 'heroic efforts to preserve human dignity on the night side of modernity and the underside of modernity' (Yancy, 1998e, p. 39). Such efforts are not carried out by monadic subjects, but within the context of a shared community, a shared sense of we-experiences that ground a sense of dynamic community. Harris is critical of thinking about African-American philosophers as constituting a community through a specifically shared *philosophical* vocabulary. After all, there are philosophers of African descent who are Marxists, existentialists, phenomenologists, and pragmatists who conceptually dwell within different and conflicting discourse communities. Yet, Harris argues that there is an overriding aim which African-American philosophers share that constitutes them as a community. It is the engagement 'in the common project to defeat the heinous consequences of racism. That's the kind of community that it is ... that binds them together regardless of their philosophy.' (Yancy, 1998g, p. 216). Indeed, it is the kind of community that avoids abstract pretentiousness, de-contextualized assumptions regarding what constitutes a philosophical problem, and the bad faith of claiming to be able to conceptualize the world from nowhere, from a site of non-perspectival, value neutrality. African-American philosophers engage (self-consciously) in philosophical endeavors that are inextricably linked to the social world through the *mediation of the body* which, as I have argued, is precisely the site of white anti-Black hatred and vilification. Yet, it is through this embodied pain and suffering that a specific epistemic capacity is installed.

As intimated above, African-American philosophy offers insights through a dynamic form of second-sight (Dubois, 45) that speaks *parrhesia* vis-à-vis Western philosophy, which is inextricably linked to the normative structure of whiteness. As Devonya N. Havis (2013) writes, 'In taking up the parrhesiastic attitude, one's actions disrupt the familiar by introducing a critique that calls attention to something that escapes the normal register' (p. 55). Through its performance of the 'god-trick' (that is, pretentions of seeing the world from nowhere) and in terms of its production of ignorance, that involves blinkers that *produce* forms of knowing incorrectly, Western philosophy obfuscates its historical and contextual contingency. African- American philosophy offers second-sight as a measure in terms of which Western philosophy can better recognize its productive ignorance. From the insights of African-American philosophy, white philosophers—that is, those who have come *to construct* Western philosophy as *the* mirror of reality—can begin to nurture a form of white double consciousness, which, in this case, is learning to see the problematic nature of their philosophical idols and metaphors. Seeing the world through the lens of African-American philosophy is meant to be dangerous; it is meant to be unsafe. It is to undermine Western philosophy's predication upon the lie that it is philosophy qua philosophy. The objective is to provide philosophers who have been blinded by occidental philosophical hegemony with what I call a gift. Not all gifts are free of discomfort. Indeed, some gifts are heavy laden with tremendous responsibility. Yet, it is a gift that ought to engender a sense of gratitude, a sense of humility, and an opportunity to give thanks —not the sort of attitude that re-inscribes Western philosophical arrogance and messianic imperialism. To give thanks is to be receptive; it is to engage in what I call a process of un-suturing (Yancy, p. 2015). Within this context, un-suturing is a process of being open to have one's historical and cultural philosophical foundations shaken, though not through hyperbolic doubt, but through *dwelling near* those African-American philosophical voices that have come to recognize the terror of Occidental philosophical practices, practices that continue to be fundamentally silent about its own racist philosophical assumptions and history, its cultural conceit, and the question of Black suffering and trauma in a world of white anti-Black racism. White double consciousness offers insights not only into its philosophical narrowness, and encourages a profound generative sense of self-alienation, but also its complicity with the denigration of Black bodies. In this gift, lies the opportunity for Western philosophy to know itself. As Sartre notes,

> Our victims know us by their scars and by their chains, and it is this that makes their evidence irrefutable. It is enough that they show us what we have made of them for us to realize what we have made of ourselves. (Fanon 1963, p. 13)

And if this is true, then Western philosophy, its white racial ethos, has made of itself a monster, something fraudulent, immoral, and unable to see so much of its own conceptual decay.

Notes

1. The reader will note that while I use the terms Black and African-American interchangeably, it is my position that 'Black,' as a marker of identity, is broader than the term African-American, especially given the fact that 'Black' includes people who are not African-American.
2. See *Critical Affinities: Nietzsche and African American Thought*, eds. Jacqueline Scott and Todd Franklin, (New York: State University of New York Press, 2006).
3. I would like thank philosopher Clarence S. Johnson for suggesting that the negative/positive distinction that I draw here be made more explicit.

References

Allen Jr., N. R. (1991). Leonard Harris on the life and work of Alain Locke. In N. R. Allen Jr. (Ed.), *African-American humanism: An anthology* (pp. 269–275). Amherst, MA: Prometheus Books.

Cone, J. H. (1986/1990). *A Black theology of liberation*. New York, NY: Orbis Books.

Descartes, R. (1637/1998). *Discourse on method and meditations on first philosophy* (D. A. Cress, Trans.). Indianapolis, IN: Hackett Publishing.

Douglass, F. (1993). *Narrative of the life of Frederick Douglass, an American slave, written by himself*. Edited with an introduction by. W. David Blight. New York, NY: Bedford/St. Martin's.

DuBois, W. E. B. (1903/1982). *The Souls of black folk*. New York, NY: New American Library.

Ellison, R. (1947/1995). *Invisible man*. New York, NY: Vintage Books.

Fanon, F. (1963). *The wretched of the earth*. New York, NY: Grove Press.

Fanon, F. (1967). *Black skin, white masks* (C. L. Markmann, Trans.). New York, NY: Grove Press.

Gray, C. H. (1996). The game of science: As played by Jean-François Lyotard. *Studies in History and Philosophy of Science Part A, 27*, 367–380.

Harris, L. (1983). Introduction. In L. Harris (Ed.), *Philosophy born of struggle: Afro-American philosophy from 1917* (pp. 1–22). Dububue, IA: Kendall/Hunt.

Havis, D. (2013). The parrhesiastic enterprise of black philosophy. *The Black Scholar, 33*, 52–58.

Hord, F. L. (Mzee Lasana Okpara), & Lee, J. S. (1995). I am because we are: An Introduction to black philosophy. In F. L. Hord & J. S. Lee (Eds.), *I am because we are: reading in black philosophy* (pp. 1–20). Amherst: University of Massachusetts Press.

Mills, C. W. (1998). *Blackness visible: Essays on philosophy and race*. Ithaca, NY: Cornell University Press.

Natanson, M. (1970). *The Journeying self: A study in philosophy and social role*. Reading, MA: Addison-Wesley.

Nietzsche, F. (1963/1966). *Beyond good and evil* (W. Kaufmann, Trans.). New York, NY: Random House, Vintage Books.

Nietzsche, F. (1989). *On the genealogy of morals*. New York, NY: Vintage.

Outlaw, L. (1996). *On Philosophy and race*. New York, NY: Routledge.

Roberts, D. (1997/1999). *Killing the black body: Race, reproduction, and the meaning of liberty*. New York, NY: Vintage Books.

Sartwell, C. (1998). *Act like you know: African-American autobiography and white identity*. Chicago, IL: University of Chicago Press.

Scott, J., & Franklin, T. (2006). *Critical affinities: Nietzsche and African American thought*. New York: State University of New York Press.

Sharpley-Whiting, T. D. (2005). Thanatic pornography, interracial rape, and the Ku Klux Klan. In T. L. Lott & J. P. Pittman (Eds.), *A companion to African-American philosophy* (pp. 407–412). Malden, MA: Blackwell Publishing.

West, C. (1982). *Prophesy deliverance: An Afro-American revolutionary christianity*. Philadelphia, PA: The Westminster Press.

West, C. (1995). The Black underclass and black philosophers. In F. L. Hord (Mzee Lasana Okpara) & J. S. Lee (Eds.), *I am because we are: Reading in black philosophy* (pp. 356–366). Amherst: University of Massachusetts Press.

West, C. (2005). Philosophy and the Afro-American experience. In T. L. Lott & J. P. Pittman (Eds.), *A companion to African-American philosophy* (pp. 7–32). Malden, MA: Blackwell.

Yancy, G. (1998a). Adrian M. S. Piper. In G. Yancy (Ed.), *African-American philosophers, 17 conversations* (pp. 49–71). New York, NY: Routledge.

Yancy, G. (1998b). Albert Mosely. In G. Yancy (Ed.), *African-American philosophers, 17 conversations* (pp. 139–162). New York, NY: Routledge.

Yancy, G. (1998c). Angela Y. Davis. In G. Yancy (Ed.), *African-American philosophers, 17 conversations* (pp. 13–30). New York, NY: Routledge.
Yancy, G. (1998d). Anita L. Allen. In G. Yancy (Ed.), *African-American philosophers, 17 conversations* (pp. 163–185). New York, NY: Routledge.
Yancy, G. (1998e). Cornel West. In G. Yancy (Ed.), *African-American philosophers, 17 conversations)* (pp. 31–48). New York, NY: Routledge.
Yancy, G. (1998f). Laurence Thomas. In G. Yancy (Ed.), *African-American philosophers, 17 conversations* (pp. 287–305). New York, NY: Routledge.
Yancy, G. (1998g). Leonard Harris. In G. Yancy (Ed.), *African-American philosophers, 17 conversations* (pp. 207–227). New York, NY: Routledge.
Yancy, G. (1998h). Lewis R. Gordon. In G. Yancy (Ed.), *African-American philosophers, 17 conversations* (pp. 95–118). New York, NY: Routledge.
Yancy, G. (1998i). Michelle M. Moody-Adams. In G. Yancy (Ed.), *African-American philosophers, 17 conversations* (pp. 119–137). New York, NY: Routledge.
Yancy, G. (1998j). Robert E. Birt. In G. Yancy (Ed.), *African-American philosophers, 17 conversations* (pp. 343–358). New York, NY: Routledge.
Yancy, G. (2008). Situated black women's voices in/on the profession of philosophy. *Hypatia: A Journal of Feminist Philosophy, 23*, 155–189.
Yancy, G. (2015). Un-Sutured. In G. Yancy (Ed.), *White self-criticality beyond anti-racism: How does it feel to be a white problem?* Edited with introduction by George Yancy (pp. xi–xxvii). Lanham, MD: Lexington Books.

How Can We Overcome the Dichotomy that Western Culture has Created Between the Concepts of Independence and Dependence?

ZEHAVIT GROSS

UNESCO Chair for Values Education, Tolerance and Peace Education, School of Education, Bar-Ilan University

Abstract

The purpose of this article, inspired by the works of Martin Buber, is to propose an alternative to the inherent dichotomy of Western culture. It may allow Western culture to transcend its fixed nature towards new directions and to suggest challenging solutions for reshaping the questions – what is the role of man in the world, and what is the nature of education? Although Western culture sacralizes and attributes pivotal importance to the independence of human beings, in actuality the human spirit contains a constant dialectic between the need for independence in shaping and crystallizing man's individualism, and his need for differentiation and dependence on otherness. While that otherness expresses defamiliarization, it also allows connections and the need to structure otherness; and dependence on it is one of the basic needs of human existence.

One of the central traits of Western culture is rational analytic thinking that enables the cerebral use of science and technology. Western culture excels in positioning individuals at the center. Unlike the Oriental culture that prevailed in ancient times until the spread across the world of the Roman culture, in which individuals are perceived as ruled by and dependent on powerful and lofty nature, in the Western perception the individual is an autonomous creature that controls nature. As a result of the sense that man's power was unlimited and man rules over everything, for centuries that proud Western culture was pervaded by philosophical blindness, because it perceives as dichotomous the concepts of independence and dependence—terms that contradict each other and cannot coexist. This perception has had far-reaching ramifications on the way in which Western culture perceives the nature of education. The purpose of this article, inspired by the works of Martin Buber, is to propose an alternative to the inherent dichotomy of Western culture. It may allow Western culture to transcend its fixed nature toward new directions and to suggest challenging solutions for reshaping the questions—what is the role of man in the world, and what is the nature of education?

A Constant Dialectic Between Dependence and Independence

Although Western culture sacralizes and attributes pivotal importance to the independence of human beings, in actuality the human spirit contains a constant dialectic between the need for independence in shaping and crystallizing man's individualism, and his need for differentiation and dependence on otherness. While that otherness expresses defamiliarization, it also allows connections and the need to structure otherness; and dependence on it is one of the basic needs of human existence. That dialectic produces four possible types of affinity that match the four types of relationship

	Independence	
Dependence	Substantial	Slight
Substantial	Autonomy	Suffocation
Slight	Liberation	Alienation

patterns between human beings (Gross, 2012), as shown in the table below:

The table presents the four types of affinity that are generated in the encounter between dependence and independence:

1. Slight independence and substantial dependence create suffocation
2. Substantial independence and slight dependence create liberation
3. Substantial independence and substantial dependence create autonomy
4. Slight independence and slight dependence create alienation

The first two situations are relatively simple and easily understood, but autonomy and alienation are complex circumstances that deserve deeper thought. These two types of affinity can be found in the philosophy of Martin Buber: Autonomy is a reality that recalls the 'I-Thou' relationship which he describes in his philosophy, while the reality of alienation recalls the 'I-It' relationship. In educational research, Buber's philosophy has chiefly been discussed from the perspective of dialog. My intention here is to analyze it from a slightly different perspective, aimed at clarifying what exactly is that affinity that Buber sought, and how it links up to the bias and blindness inherent in the Western outlook.

According to Buber, the world of the 'It' is an alienated one: 'When left to itself, the world of the 'It' becomes alienated and is taken over by demons and spirits' (Buber, 1973, p. 47). Buber explains the self's basic need for dependence as follows: 'The "I" is imbued with affinity, and when it exists beyond it, is held by a strong golden thread on which changing situations are strung.' Lack of dependence engenders alienation and transforms nearby others into 'them' (ibid.). In the reality of the 'It,' the question of independence does not exist at all, because it is a priori alienated, and independence is a demarcating act that is performed through affinity with others: 'A creature's "I" becomes visible when he demarcates his own area in terms of other independent creatures' (p. 48).

In 'I-Thou' relations, the question of dependence is a substantive and fundamental one: 'the purpose of the affinity is its selfhood, and it is: the contact with the Thou. Because during contacts with others, we are touched by the breath of the "Thou," and of eternal life … one who is imbued with and stands in affinities participates in one of all the realities. That is: he participates in an experience that does not depend on him alone, and does not exist for him alone' (p. 49). The 'I' exists because it participates in reality, and it is that absolute dependence on affinity with the 'Thou' that makes it possible to participate in reality.

Buber explains that dependence of the 'I' on the 'Thou' does not result in man losing his independence: On the contrary, his 'subjectivity' is empowered and nurtured due to the dependence: 'But when the "I" abandons affinity enters into detachment abandonment and grows aware of this, his reality is not diminished. Participation remains inherent within him … And, this is the sovereignty of subjectivity, where the "I" grows aware of his simultaneous connection and abandonment. One does not see true subjectivity, but a dynamic perception, in the sense of the jolted "I" within its isolating truth' (ibid).

He emphasizes that in order to achieve independence and differentiation, man paradoxically needs both dependence and a passion for affinity: 'this is also the place where the passion for affinity is born, soaring higher and higher, seeking full partnership in the experience. With subjectivity, the spiritual selfhood of the personality matures and develops' (ibid.).

Independence allows the 'I' to recognize itself, recalling 'thus, here I am' and out of recognition with his 'thusness,' as Buber phrased it, the 'I' can connect up to the 'Thou'. Therefore, the ideal 'I-Thou' encounter is created in conditions of both substantial dependence and substantial independence. The 'Thou' that Buber speaks of is the eternal 'Thou:' 'the elongated lines of the affinities meet each other in the eternal Thou' (p. 57). Buber continues and argues that, 'Human beings give many names to their eternal Thou … however, all the names of God retain their holiness … since everyone who talks of God and in his heart truly intends to the "Thou," is in fact naming … the true Thou of his life, that contains all the other affinities' (pp. 57–58).

When the Almighty expelled Adam and Eve from the Garden of Eden, he also punished the serpent whose punishment was '… upon thy belly shalt thou go, and dust shalt thou eat all the days of thy life' (Genesis, 3, 14). We learn from this that the serpent's punishment was that the Almighty released him from dependence on Him, since its food would always be available (unlike all the other creatures that depend on G-d for their existence). It is dependence that renders human beings human, and the 'serpent-like quality' within humans erupts when they believe they no longer need others and are freed from dependence.

Dependence and independence are inverse forms and types of relations, and in the absence of these two situations—when man is not in a state of dependence but also has no option for the independence that is awarded through affinity and context—a reality of alienation and indifference takes shape. The possibility defined in the table above as autonomy, actually reflects the most balanced and desirable situation.

Between Independence and Dependence—The Divine Sanctuary within Man

Western culture has failed to understand that empowering man's natural independence and empowering his natural dependence on a supreme moral compass—and finding the balance between the two—are precisely what makes possible man's unmediated encounter with the divine and sublime within him. Revealing the divine in the human means laying bare the facets that connect up man's will and needs for independence with his need for dependence on God as a source of morality and exaltation. Human authenticity is found at that point where a person chooses and defines his independence and his dependence on God. That conscious choice, in fact, structuring G-d in the domain of the spirit.

We read in the Torah 'And let them make me a sanctuary; that I may dwell among them' (Exodus, 25, 8). On the face of it, this should read 'And I dwelt within them' but the Torah commands us to undertake a long process of structuring the personal inner sanctuary in which G-d will dwell—a process in which the transcendent G-d becomes the immanent G-d. This process must be the very heart of education. Man is the realm in which G-d dwells, and through man, he is revealed to be the whole of reality.

One of the central questions with which theology engages is: 'where can we find G-d?' is there a specific, concrete site of holiness, or is 'the whole Earth His glory'? The question of God's location is connected, I believe, to the question 'where art thou?' that G-d asked Adam after he sinned in the Garden of Eden. The man who hid himself from G-d did not allow Him to dwell within him—God looked for the 'sanctuary' but Adam fled from him and from his G-d. Rabbi Abraham Isaac Kook HaCohen wrote in his *Orot ha'kodesh*: that 'Man's first sin was ignoring his selfhood by listening to the serpent and did not know how to reply clearly to the question 'where art thou?' because he was overcome by losing his selfhood (his 'I') (Kook HaCohen, 1964, Part 3, Kam-Kama). The first man sinned in that—instead of behaving naturally—he listened to the voice of the serpent, which represents the external and extrinsic, and ate from the tree of knowledge. As a result, he covered himself with clothes and outer layers. Because of those clothes, which cover what is natural, he was unable to answer the question 'where art thou?' covered by those 'layers,' he lost his authentic natural self (his 'selfhood,' as the author wrote).

It is the inspiration of the divine presence and its embodiment within man that allows man on the one hand to create and produce, and, on the other hand, requires him to diminish himself and submit to his human limitations—which implies dependence. And that inspiration requires him to 'peel off' that external layer, removing what conceals him and thus disclosing what is 'natural' within man. Man's purpose in the world is to discover his natural power that authentic power which exists within him, without any external layers and artifice. His principal aim in being distinct from animals is to construct a sanctuary for the divine presence, for high and noble moral powers, within him. And, this must also be the aim of education; the objective that young learners will be able to answer the question 'where art thou?'—in other words, where are you positioned in your process of seeking the divine within you, in building a sanctuary for the divine presence and morality within you?

The Nature of Education: The Quest for Autonomy and Affinity

The balance between the dependence–independence relation generates a new essence, where dependence no longer expresses coercion but intention. Frankenstein (1977) discussed this possibility, distinguishing between freedom (which is liable to degenerate into lawlessness and from there to anarchy) and coercion (which he sees a priori as unacceptable). He proposed that the alternative is intention and thus granting autonomy within the structure of authority relationships is not total freedom, but rather individualist growth and development from a person's affinity with a set of values and the intentional position of an educating figure, on which she or he is dependent.

According to Buber, education is grounded on a quest and intention toward autonomy, and it entails a constant dialectic between relations of dependence and independence. The educator's role is to direct students to find the appropriate amount and balance between dependence and independence, so as to create meaningful I-Thou relations. The nature of education, he contends, is to generate affinities—between man and himself, between man and his G-d, and man and society.

Buber stresses that creating affinity is a long spiritual process and that affinity must be dialogic, an affinity containing mutuality and friendship, that 'encompasses a genuine interaction between souls' (Buber, 1973, p. 258). Buber speaks of the duality that man senses in the process of creating affinity and communication, when he experiences 'the boundary of otherness and the grace inherent in communicating with the other' (Buber, p. 258). The boundary of otherness—is the distinct autonomous personality, and the sense of grace generated by the acknowledging of his unusual dependence on the other, whom he transforms in a spiritual process from 'It' to 'Thou.'

The nature of education has to be the creation of an I-Thou affinity: its overarching aim is an unmediated encounter with G-d—the eternal 'I.' Maturity and readiness for that special encounter of the 'I-Thou' and the capacity to uphold the affinity with 'I-Thou' requires purification, and peeling away the outer layers. The educating process is therefore one of clarifying, purifying, distilling, reducing the 'I' until one finds the essential place of the divine within man. The encounter with G-d is a meeting with the positive creative and productive powers within the individual's personality, and they are capable of building a world in its entirety, and ultimately of achieving *tikkun olam*—repairing the world.

Education means 'repairing the world through the kingdom of G-d'—spiritual labor that purifies the individual. Repairing the world through the kingdom of G-d, a phrase which appears in the *Siddur*—the Jewish prayer book is more than just repairing the world in its socialist meaning. It means repairing a broken vessel (the world) a task which can only be performed if it is done by people acting in 'G-d's image.' In the prayer books of Yemenite Jews, inspired by the prayers of the Rambam (Maimonides), one prayer exhorts us, in a play on Hebrew words, to 'design' (not 'repair') the kingdom of G-d. In other words, to plan and establish the world, to design a world from the place where man connects to his G-d. This is the special dialectic and affinity between dependence and independence, between 'I' and 'Thou.' This is a new cosmic reorganization of the concepts *controller* and *controlled* that contradicts their accepted meaning in classic Western thought. It is spiritual labor, a lifetime project that allows man, in a continuing process of choice, to choose to be a man distinct from animal. This is principally achieved by finding a balance between dependence and independence, and from there to discover 'selfhood' in the language of Rabbi Kook, in all its beauty and splendor, when he assumes the form of G-d above. That approach allows modern man to rise beyond the fixed Western concepts, toward a trajectory of cerebral and conscious choice of the noble and lofty, and to become an integral part of it.

References

Buber, M. M. (1973). *Besod Siach. Ktavim Philosophiim* [The dialogue on man and being. Philosophical writings]. (Vol. 1). Jerusalem: Bialik Institute [Hebrew].

Frankenstein, K. (1977). *Kenut va'shivyon: hirhurim shel psicholog u'mehanech* [Education-core and Essence]. Tel Aviv: Sifriat Poalim [Hebrew].

Gross, Z. (2012). The nature of education: Creating an affinity between man and his god. In A. Freiman & I. Tadmor (Eds.), *Hinuch, mahut va'ruach* [Education-core and Essence]. MOFET Institute: Tel Aviv [Hebrew].

Kook HaCohen, A. I. (1964). *Orot ha'kodesh* [Ha'Orot: The illuminations of Rav Kook Tz'l]. (Vol. 3). Jerusalem: Mossad Harav Kook [Hebrew].

Rethinking the 'Western Tradition'

PENNY ENSLIN[a] & KAI HORSTHEMKE[b]
[a]*School of Education, University of Glasgow;* [b]*School of Education, University of the Witwatersrand*

Abstract

In recent years, the 'Western tradition' has increasingly come under attack in anti-colonialist and postmodernist discourses. It is not difficult to sympathise with the concerns that underlie advocacy of historically marginalised traditions, and the West undoubtedly has a lot to answer for. Nonetheless, while arguing a qualified yes to the central question posed for this special issue, we question the assumption that the West can be neatly distinguished from alternative traditions of thought. We argue that there is fundamental implicit and explicit agreement across traditions about the most difficult of issues and on standards about how to reason about them and that the 'West' has demonstrably learned from within and without itself. But, we question the very viability under conditions of heightened globalisation and neo-colonialism of distinguishing between thought of the 'West' and thought outside the West. It is time to move beyond the reified assumptions that underlie the idea of 'Western thought', cast as an agent with a collective purpose.

Introduction

In recent years, the 'Western (or Northern) tradition' has increasingly come under attack, in anti-colonialist and postmodernist discourses. Thus, the targeted tradition has on different occasions been labelled 'mechanistic, materialistic, reductionistic, empirical, rational, decontextualized, mathematically idealised, ... ideological, masculine, elitist, competitive, exploitive, and violent' (Aikenhead, 1997, p. 5, 1996, pp. 9, 10, 2001, pp. 11, 12). Similar attributes of the nature of 'Western' science and knowledge[1] ('mechanistic', 'reductivist', 'exclusionist' and 'particularistic'; as opposed to the 'holism' of indigenous or traditional thinking and world views) are rehearsed by Russell Bishop (1998), Semali and Kincheloe (1999), Goduka (2000), and Fatnowna and Pickett (2002). In Glen Aikenhead's characterisation of 'Aboriginal' or 'First Nations knowledge of nature', it 'contrasts with Western scientific knowledge in a number of ways':

- 'in their social goals: survival of a people *versus* the luxury of gaining knowledge for the sake of knowledge and for power over nature and other people';
- 'in intellectual goals: to co-exist with mystery in nature by celebrating mystery *versus* to eradicate mystery by explaining it away';
- 'in their association with human action: intimately and subjectively interrelated *versus* formally and objectively decontextualised';
- 'holistic First Nations perspectives with their gentle, accommodating, intuitive, and spiritual wisdom, *versus* reductionist Western science with its aggressive, manipulative, mechanistic, and analytical explanations'; and finally
- 'in their basic concepts of time: circular for Aboriginals, rectilinear for scientists' (Aikenhead, 1997, pp. 5–6).

Although Aikenhead's characterisation of the 'subculture of science' appears to be little more than caricature and tendentious demonisation, on a par with the essentialising nonsense of those who arrogantly dismiss the possibility of non-occidental contributions to knowledge and scientific research and inquiry, and despite his manifest romanticisation of the indigene, it is not difficult to sympathise with the concerns that underlie advocacy of historically marginalised traditions. The West has undoubtedly much to answer for. To begin with, significant quanta of Western knowledge, science, technology and 'rationality' have led to, or have had as a significant goal, the subjugation of nature and so far have been devastatingly efficient. The pursuit of nuclear energy, wholesale environmental degradation, deforestation and destruction of flora and fauna, factory farming of non-human animals for human consumption, vivisection, and genetic engineering and manipulation are deplorable and—indeed—irrational. Moreover, the marginalisation and inferiorisation of indigenous peoples' practices, skills and insights has, to a large extent, been arrogant and of similarly questionable rationality. The ravages and lingering consequences of colonialism, oppression and subjugation attest to the cruel efficiency of a vast number of Western (-sponsored) practices. Current attempts by economically, industrially and technologically dominant nations to (re)colonise or appropriate for commercial gain these practices, skills and insights are exploitive and contemptible. Finally, certain traditional streams of Western thought have underpinned colonial and neo-colonial educational practices and systems. Historically, these have lain at the heart of the cultural consequences of colonialism, in curricula that assumed the truth and greater importance of Western forms of knowledge, denigrating and marginalising so-called indigenous epistemologies and educational traditions.

Nonetheless, there may be serious misconceptions and indeed biases at work in the unqualified targeting of 'the Western tradition'. We, the authors of this article find binary opposition often useful, for reasons of conceptual clarity, amongst many other things. In this case, however, we reject the 'binaries' involved in the topic set for the special edition of this journal. We do not buy into the 'problem' as it is posed here. However, our responses to the questions posed for the special issue ('Does the Western tradition have the intellectual resources to overcome its philosophical blindnesses?'; 'Can it learn from, by, despite, itself?'; 'Does it have the capacity to learn from other traditions?') are reservedly affirmative, and we have distinct considered intuitions regarding the resources (of the tradition in question) required for this kind of learning. However plausible the charge of 'philosophical blindness' may sometimes be, there are several considerations that it would be foolish to ignore. Firstly, like its critics, Western thought is diverse and no longer neatly distinguishable from alternative traditions. There are no easy boundaries between 'the West' and 'the rest'. Secondly, despite disagreement, there is a shared implicit assumption among all *plausible* views of the possibility of discussion and argument about even the most difficult ontological, epistemological and ethical issues. Thirdly, there appears to exist basic agreement on some standard of good and bad reasoning about ontological, epistemological and ethical matters in education, as in other areas of public concern and intellectual life. Fourthly, thought in the West has demonstrably both produced searching internal critique and also engaged with criticism from without, although such boundaries have become increasingly porous. Finally, we argue, fifthly, that a preoccupation with putative Western ideas as a target for resistance in contemporary educational theory mischaracterises contemporary neo-colonial forces and their significance.

Of 'Blind Spots' and 'Blank Spots'

As has been evident in the discussion of Aikenhead above, many friends of the 'subaltern' pit their preferred orientation against a straw-person that is swiftly and summarily dispensed with. This kind of move also informs common invocation of the Western tradition's 'philosophical blindnesses'. Referring to 'two generic forms that … ignorance can take' (Wagner, 2003, p. 16), Jon Wagner claims that 'blind spots and bank spots are at the core of *all* research endeavours' (Wagner, 2003, p. 19):

> All scientists [including philosophers and educational researchers] operate in a world defined by what they think and know to be true. What they don't know well enough to even ask about or care about are their *blind spots*. What they know enough to question but not to answer are their *blank spots*. The same phenomenal categories are alive for nonscientists as well, and in some ways the particulars of those categories for scientists and nonscientists have much in common. (Wagner, 2003, p. 16; emphasis added)

Lesley le Grange, following Wagner, refers to blank spots and blind spots as 'two kinds of ignorance produced by *Western* knowledge systems', in particular (Le Grange, 2004, p. 69; emphasis added), especially in their hegemonic domination vis-à-vis 'marginalised epistemologies'(Le Grange, 2004, p. 70) and 'indigenous ways of knowing' (Le Grange, 2004, p. 71).

> Critiques of Western knowledge by feminists, sociologists of knowledge and post-colonialists operating within Western research traditions could be interpreted as shifting *blind spots* to *blank spots*—critiquing Western ways of knowing [is] now becoming part of the dialogues and conversations of Western scholars. This reflexive response is encouraging and opens up spaces for greater recognition of indigenous knowledges. However, the Western cultural archive produces blind spots, aspects that *Western scholars will not know enough about or care about*. (Le Grange, 2004, p. 74; emphasis added)

It would appear, then, that Le Grange's view, more or less explicitly, involves a negative response to the questions guiding the theme of this special issue of EPAT. In the context of the present discussion, he seems to acknowledge too little here and rules out the possibility of further engagement.

It is a common sociological sleight of hand to observe that the position authors critical of 'other'/'subaltern' ways of knowing or science traditions

> is disturbingly devoid of self-reflexivity. There is no evidence of a consciousness of how their race and class positions them, and of how the Western discourses they have taken up in their educational journeys (have) dispose (d) them to work in particular ways, and also of the blind spots their ways of researching/writing create. (Le Grange, 2005, p. 137)

It is not unusual for those who are critical of politically correct stances and of glorification of the indigene or aboriginal to be accused of manifesting 'imperialist tendencies' (Le Grange, 2005, p. 128), of race- and class-based prejudice.

However plausible the charge of 'philosophical blindness' against the 'Western tradition' may sometimes be, and from a historical perspective has often been, there are nonetheless several considerations that it would be foolish to ignore.

How the West was Never 'One': The Responses

1. Like its critics, Western thought is diverse and no longer neatly distinguishable from alternative traditions. The 'Western tradition' is not (any longer) characteristically or paradigmatically the 'Enlightenment tradition' or the 'analytical tradition'. It incorporates a multitude of different philosophical perspectives and traditions: pragmatism, interpretivism, phenomenology and hermeneutics, critical theory, the different kinds of feminism and postmodernism, and critical realism, to name only a few. These perspectives and traditions are characterised not only by an openness and proximity to (self-)critique (we return to this point below) but also by brisk and tireless 'border crossings'.

We take Edward Said's *Orientalism* (1978/2003) as exemplifying several of our claims about Western thought. This foundational postcolonial text is not merely a devastating expose of the ways in which this thread in post-Enlightenment Western thought managed Orientalist representations of the Oriental as other, as an expression of the power of the coloniser over the colonised. Describing himself as 'speaking both as an American and as an Arab' (Said, 1978/2003, p. xxvi), Said wrote as a Palestinian but from within the Western academy, drawing on the ideas of a range of Western scholars that included Foucault, Gramsci and—ambiguously—Marx. With Orientalism now widely acknowledged, not least in the West itself, as one of the most shameful episodes in the history of Western learning, this text and the postcolonial literature that has burgeoned since its publication surely constitute evidence that the West, if there is still or ever was such an intentional entity, can and has learned from historical errors, overcoming such blindnesses. Globalisation of academic exchange and discourse, with scholars and ideas crossing geographic and intellectual borders with increasing ease and frequency, prompts the question of how any area of global thought could possibly learn by itself any more. None of these observations should be taken as assuming that sites of Western thought have yet sufficiently accommodated non-Western thought or that critique of Western traditions of thought is yet complete.

2. Despite disagreement, there is a shared implicit assumption among all *plausible* views of the possibility of discussion and argument about even the most difficult ontological, epistemological and ethical issues. For one thing, this explains why many views are articulated in implicit or explicit conversation with theoretical adversaries. In 'implicit conversation', one has the adversaries 'in mind': these range from straw persons dispensed with in an easy and swift demolition job (a move that would not make one's own, favoured position any stronger; for examples of this strategy, see Aikenhead, 1997, pp. 5–6, 1996, pp. 9, 10, 2001, pp. 11, 12) to imagining and carefully dealing with the strongest possible opposition to one's stance (a move that is often arguably likely to strengthen the latter; see, for example, Carr, 2006, pp. 151–154).[2] 'Explicit conversation' concerns engagement with (and usually opposition to) views that have actually been articulated by 'real' theoretical opponents (e.g. Carr, 2006, p. 151; Le Grange, 2005, p. 137). For another, the confidence placed in the possibility of discussion and argument about difficult philosophical issues in education (as in other areas of inquiry) is exemplified in the writings of those who criticise 'traditional research epistemologies' of the 'Western world' on the grounds of Western educational researchers' 'preoccupation with neutrality, objectivity and distance', and who then go on to argue the case for indigenous people's 'participation in the construction, validation, and legitimization of knowledge' (Bishop, 1998, pp. 200–201). While these sorts of exchanges (that characteristically happen at conferences on indigenous knowledge systems, ethnomathematics and the like) often assume the form of 'preaching to the converted', the deeper intention is surely to win over a few converts from the other camp. In other words, more often than not, the aim of this kind of argumentation is to make a compelling (impersonal, objective, universally valid) case for one's favoured position.

3. There appears to exist basic agreement on some standard of good reasoning about ontological, epistemological and ethical matters in education, as in other areas of public concern and intellectual life. Whatever else may be said about the practical effectiveness of philosophy of education, it is surely true that serious and committed philosophical thinkers and practitioners of most if not all persuasions are 'committed to following through the implications of rational argument and … impersonal rational principles (commitment to truth, impartiality, respect for evidence and the like)' (Carr, 2004, p. 56). It is surely also true that they would like their arguments and principles to appear uncorrupted 'by a combination of irrational influences such as political expediency, vested interests and established power' (Carr, 2004, p. 56).

Whether or not these considerations have a peculiarly 'Western' origin, they are ignored by 'other traditions' and approaches to education that might be based on them, at the peril of the latter.

4. The Western tradition is not only diverse and increasingly overlapping with others. Indeed, much of the critique of the worst of western thought has come from within the 'West'. As Le Grange concedes, citing the contributions of sociology of

knowledge, feminist scholarship and postcolonial thought, extensive critique of 'Western ways of knowing' (Le Grange, 2004, p. 74) has taken place within the traditions of Western research. To these examples can be added Critical Theory's extended and often searing criticism of the intellectual tradition of Enlightenment modernity, exemplified in Theodor Adorno and Max Horkheimer's description of the world under western modernity, as 'disaster triumphant' (1979, p. 3). Instead of liberating human beings, they argue, instrumental reason is irrational, culminating in Nazi death camps and a capitalist system that commodifies through the market, including and especially in the culture industry.

While such critiques were written from within the West, however, and as postmodern and postcolonial critique grew, they have become less easy to locate in relation to a clear intellectual and geographical context. Said's work not only crosses borders, critiquing Orientalism by exposing its failings and drawing in postcolonial understandings while emphasising hybridity, warning against characterisations of cultures as distinct, homogeneous and monolithic. Said also advises against the assumption (which lies of course at the heart of Orientalist thinking) that terms like 'Orient' or 'West' are ontologically stable, as both are fictions, products of human effort, organised and open to manipulation. Said himself declares a preference for careful analysis and critique aimed at understanding as against knowledge that is 'part of an overall campaign of self-affirmation, belligerency and outright war' (Said, 1978/2003, p. xix) and 'bursts of polemical, thought-stopping fury that so imprison us in labels and antagonistic debate whose goal is a belligerent, collective identity rather than understanding and intellectual exchange' (Said, 1978/2003, p. xxii).

5. There are wider implications than this to Said's cautions about simplistic binaries between thought that is supposedly of the West and of the rest. The 'blind spots' that arise from focusing too heavily on 'the classical period' of the society or language that is being studied, fixing them 'for all time, for ontological reasons that no empirical material can dislodge or alter' (Said, 1978/ 2003, p. 70), has further consequences, to which we now turn.

Conceptions of 'thought' as fixed geographically and in time can imprison us in analytical categories that overemphasise ahistorical conceptions of colonialism and culture. Arif Dirlik argues that preoccupation with the cultural legacies of colonialism distracts attention from what is distinctive about contemporary colonialism: 'its relationship to capitalism' (Dirlik, 2002, p. 428). This lends exaggerated importance to the past and promotes obliviousness to how power has been reconstructed by globalised capitalism.

Dirlik observes how the relationship between coloniser and colonised has tended to be understood in Manichean terms, as opposed to one another, cast in terms of race, underplaying the cultural entanglement between the two, bound together in a structural dialectic; and how Third World voices have demanded that the psychological and cultural aspects of colonialism be recognised, thus shifting the analytical emphasis away from 'the economic and political to the cultural and the personal experiential' (Dirlik, 2002, p. 431). So political economy has ceased to mediate in questions of culture (Dirlik, 2002, p. 432).

> Globalization returns us to a condition where once again it is capitalism, rather than colonialism, that appears as the major problem. The avoidance of this question is a serious problem of contemporary postcolonial criticism which, focused on past legacies, is largely oblivious to its own conditions of existence and its relationship to contemporary configurations of power. It also ignores the ways in which its interpretation of the past may serve to promote, or at least, play into the hands of a globalized capitalism. (Dirlik, 2002, p. 440)

No doubt indigenous people in postcolonial contexts have suffered marginalisation and oppression. However understandable the assertion of non-Western, indigenous values and epistemologies as a response to the cultural alienation caused by colonialism, overemphasising this fact can distract from recognition of the full range of such marginalisation and oppression. Colonialism's consequences are also material, in the form of growing international and intranational poverty. Furthermore, at the same time as capitalism's self-reinvention has brought former colonies into the global economy, postcolonial critics are themselves now inserted into the global intellectual elite, drawing on practices of critique largely drawn from 'Western' intellectual traditions of criticism located within traditions of cultural nationalism no less Western in origin. Particularly in education, resistance to the lingering effects of colonialism that focuses too strongly on cultural marginalisation distracts critical attention from the destruction primarily wrought by neo-liberalism, ineffectually fought by reversion to epistemic and moral traditionalism. Addressing human needs through education—including by widening policy, curricula and pedagogy with ways of knowing beyond the worst of the historical West—requires critical attention to the power and influence of global capital, the ongoing destruction wrought by industrial technology, the harnessing of education to the production of labour power to serve the interests of capital and the attendant subversion of education through the imposition of business-inspired models of management of education on its organisation.

Furthermore, and crucial to possibilities for resistance to global capitalism and its increasing influence on education global capitalism is no longer geographically confined to the West. On the contrary, with the decline of Europe and the rapid rise of Eastern giants, although the knowledge that historically underpinned Western science and technology and so their destructive effects may have been Western in origin, capitalism is hardly just 'Western' any longer (Dirlik, 2002, p. 444).

Conclusion: Beyond 'Western Thought'

While arguing a qualified affirmative answer to the key question of whether the Western tradition can overcome its blindnesses, we have acknowledged both those historical blindnesses and their destructive consequences. But, emphasising the diversity of thought in the West and its imbrication now in globalised flows of ideas that belie assumptions about geographical exclusivity, we have argued that Western thought has drawn on resources from within and without to learn, but by no means by itself. Yet, where we have used the term 'Western thought' for the sake of argument, we find this reified category no longer useful; it mistakenly assumes too that there could be a collective Western agent with both a unified sense of themselves and a collective purpose that includes a coherent single stance towards other forms of 'thought'. As long as vanguardist postcolonial leaders and intellectuals pursue a politics of resentment, in terms that Said warns against, we will remain distracted from the most virulent forces that threaten global well-being, not least in its educational systems.

Notes

1. While the concern in the examples provided here is almost exclusively with science and knowledge, and scientific epistemologies, a wider survey must surely also include political theory, anthropology, historiography, literature, aesthetics and ethics.
2. Wilfred Carr anticipates three sets of compelling responses to his postfoundationalist argument, and he attempts to defend his position against each of these, with varying degrees of success.

References

Adorno, T., & Horkheimer, M. (1979). *Dialectic of enlightenment.* London: Verso.

Aikenhead, G. S. (1996). Science education: Border crossing into the subculture of science. *Studies in Science Education, 27*, 1–52.

Aikenhead, G. S. (1997). Towards a first nations cross-cultural science and technology curriculum. *Science & Education, 81*, 217–238; 1–35. Retrieved May 1, 2012, from http://www.usask.ca/education/people/aikenhead/firstnat.pdf

Aikenhead, G. S. (2001). Integrating western and aboriginal sciences: Cross-cultural teaching. *Research in Science Education, 31*, 337–355.

Bishop, R. (1998). Freeing ourselves from neo-colonial domination in research: A Maori approach to creating knowledge. *Qualitative Studies in Education, 11*, 199–219.

Carr, W. (2004). Philosophy and education. *Journal of Philosophy of Education, 38*, 55–73.

Carr, W. (2006). Education without theory. *British Journal of Educational Studies, 54*, 136–159.

Dirlik, A. (2002). Rethinking colonialism: Globalization, postcolonialism, and the nation. *Interventions, 4*, 428–448.

Fatnowna, S., & Pickett, H. (2002). Indigenous contemporary knowledge development through research: The task for an indigenous academy. In C. Odora Hoppers (Ed.), *Indigenous knowledge and the integration of knowledge systems: Towards a philosophy of articulation* (pp. 209–236). Claremont: New Africa Books.

Goduka, I. N. (2000). African/indigenous philosophies: Legitimizing spiritually centred wisdoms within the academy. In P. Higgs, N. C. G. Vakalisa, T. V. Mda, & N. T. Assie-Lumumba (Eds.), *African voices in education* (pp. 63–83). Lansdowne: Juta.

Le Grange, L. (2004). Ignorance, trust and educational research. *Journal of Education, 33*, 69–84.

Le Grange, L. (2005). African philosophy of education: An emerging discourse in South Africa. In Y. Waghid, B. Van Wyk, F. Adams, & I. November (Eds.), *African(a) philosophy of education: Reconstructions and deconstructions* (pp. 126–139). Stellenbosch: Department of Education Policy Studies, Stellenbosch University.

Said, E. (1978/2003). *Orientalism*. Preface to the Twenty-Fifth Anniversary edition. New York, NY: Random House.

Semali, L. M., & Kincheloe, J. L. (1999). Introduction: What is indigenous knowledge and why should we study it? In L. M. Semali & J. L. Kincheloe (Eds.), *What is indigenous knowledge?: Voices from the academy* (pp. 3–57). New York, NY: Falmer Press.

Wagner, J. (2003). Ignorance in educational research: Or, how can you not know that? *Educational Researcher, 22*, 15–23.

How the West Was One: The Western as individualist, the African as communitarian

THADDEUS METZ
Department of Philosophy, University of Johannesburg

Abstract

There is a kernel of truth in the claim that Western philosophy and practice of education is individualistic; theory in Euro-America tends to prize properties that are internal to a human being, such as her autonomy, rationality, knowledge, pleasure, desires, self-esteem and self-realisation, and education there tends to adopt techniques focused on the individual placed at some distance from others. What is striking about other philosophical–educational traditions in the East and the South is that they are typically much more communitarian. I argue that since geographical terms such as 'Western', 'African' and the like are best construed as picking out properties that are salient in a region, it is fair to conclude that the Western is individualist and that the African is communitarian. What this means is that if I am correct about a noticeable contrast between philosophies of education typical in the West and in sub-Saharan Africa, and if there are, upon reflection, attractive facets of communitarianism, then those in the West and in societies influenced by it should in some real sense become less Western, in order to take them on.

It is impossible to make a general statement that covers every exception, and yet conversation so often consists of each person pointing out the obvious exceptions to the other person's statements. Hugh Prather (*Notes to Myself*)

Introduction: Approaching 'the West'

Western philosophies of education are individualist, whereas sub-Saharan African ones are communitarian.

I believe that this statement is true and that it can be sensibly asserted without committing any of the sins routinely lumped under the heading of 'essentializing', that is without indicating that all and only theories of education from Euro-America are individualist and that all and only those from below the Sahara are communitarian, and without implying that views from these locales necessarily have these respective characteristics.[1] In this article, I aim to provide a general account of how to plausibly construe geographical labels such as 'Western' and 'African', and to bring out what it entails for the way to understand different philosophies of education.

Although I reject an essentialist use of geographical labels, that does not mean that I advance a constructivist one according to which their meaning is determined merely by the properties that those in a group mentally associate with them. *Contra* the constructivist, I believe that a geographical label such as 'Western' has an objective content about which people can be mistaken, while *contra* the essentialist, I maintain that this content is not exclusive to, exhaustive of or fixed in the relevant locale. In terms familiar to those with expertise in the philosophy of language, I maintain that the referent of geographical labels is determined neither by a mere cluster of descriptions nor by rigid designation.

Appealing to my account of what terms such as 'Western' plausibly mean, I ultimately suggest that because of what I see as individualist blind spots in the Western tradition, those who adhere to Western views probably have some good reason to hold ones that are more communitarian. Although the words 'Western' and the like can be used without essentializing, it is likely the case that what is picked out by that term is too narrow for developing an attractive philosophy of education. If so, and the Western tradition has something to learn from African or more broadly communitarian perspectives, then, as I explain, the West should become less Western and should over time change what 'Western' means.

How to Construe Geographical Labels

My view about what geographical labels mean is this: they refer to features that are *salient* in a locale, at least over a substantial amount of time. They pick out properties that have for a long while been recurrent in a place in a way they have tended not to be elsewhere. They denote fairly long-standing characteristics in a region that differentiate it from many other regions.

Such a view is not constructivist, for it implies that there is a mind-independent fact of the matter about the frequency with which certain properties are present in places, about which one or one's group could be mistaken. Such a view is also not essentialist, for it does not imply that the relevant properties are to be found only in a certain location, throughout that location or invariably in it.

Consider some examples. Marsupials are Australian. That is true, I submit, even though one will find a number of marsupials in South and Central America, one will not find marsupials in downtown Sydney, and the day could come when there are no marsupials in Australia. Hence, a natural reading of the statement is not essentialist. In addition, it is not constructivist, for what makes it the case that marsupials are Australian is not merely that people believe it to be; if a group asserted that marsupials were not Australian but rather African, it would be incorrect. Instead, the claim that marsupials are Australian appears true in virtue of the objective fact that marsupials have for a long while been frequent in Australia in a way they have tended not to be elsewhere. Basically, they stand out there.

Here is another one: baseball is American. Again, I submit this claim is true, but not true 'essentially'. After all, the Cubans and Japanese are well known for playing baseball; it is course true that not all Americans play it or even appreciate it; and there is nothing preventing Americans from giving up this sport entirely. And again, the fact that baseball is American is not 'constructed', for if a sociologist of sport failed to mention baseball when aiming to provide a general account of sport in the States, she would be epistemically guilty of having made a glaring omission. Baseball is American insofar as it is salient there.

Now, let me turn to terms that are central to the topic of this article. Consider the fact that the combination of markets, science and constitutionalism is Western. That is true even though one will find it in places beyond Europe and America, such as South Africa and Australia, and even though one will not find it deep in the Amazon jungle among, say, the Yanomamo people.

Similarly, it is African to hold a belief in the need to respect ancestors, wise progenitors of a clan who have survived the death of their bodies and now live in an invisible form on earth. That is true despite the facts that far from all sub-Saharans hold this belief and that other traditions, particularly in the East, also include reverence for ancestors. What makes the label 'African' or 'sub-Saharan' apt is that a belief in ancestors is at the core of the moral and cosmological world views of a great many indigenous peoples below the Sahara.

In short, talk of things 'Western' and 'African' picks out features that are salient in these respective parts of the world,[2] which, *contra* some philosophers of education, does not mean that calling something 'African' implies that it is utterly unique to that part of the world (e.g. Horsthemke & Enslin, 2005; Parker, 2003). I believe that this what most people mean when they use such terms, in the light of the several examples above. However, if I am incorrect about that, then note that it would be quite useful if people were to use them this way. I agree that the sins of essentialism are sins, even if those who point them out tend to be too quick to cast stones. And if one were to be constructivist about these terms, then people would routinely speak past one another when they associate different properties with the same term (a familiar problem with the descriptivist or cluster theory of reference). In sum, I submit that my account of geographical labels accurately describes the way people use them or at least the way they should in order to facilitate comparison and debate.

Western and African Philosophy of Education Compared

If I am correct about how to use geographical labels, then, in order to characterise Western philosophy of education in comparison with African, I need to recount properties that are salient in these two traditions. Upon doing so, I conclude in this section that it is fair to deem the former individualist and the latter communitarian.

For a long while in the Western part of the world, that is in Europe, the UK and North America, the practices and philosophies of education have been recurrently focused on individual persons. Consider this first when it comes to the final ends sought out or prescribed. Practitioners and theorists have tended to prize properties that are internal to a human being, making no essential reference to anyone but her. I have in mind properties such as her autonomy, rationality, intellectual virtues, self-development, self-esteem, pleasure, desires and work-related abilities. It is extraordinarily common to find Western normative theorists maintaining that the ultimate aim of education should be to enable the young to judge their traditions, to think critically, to freely pursue a conception of the good, to realise themselves and so on. Individual agency has been the name of the game.

In addition, with respect to higher education, a notable element of Western approaches has been to seek out knowledge for its own sake. For instance, Aristotle (350 B.C.E.) famously rates knowledge of the cosmos as the highest to be obtained despite being 'useless' and not among 'human goods', and Edmund Husserl (1935) characterises the entire European intellectual tradition in terms of a propensity to adopt what he calls 'a purely "theoretical" attitude' that is 'thoroughly unpractical'.[3]

There have been exceptions, of course. To name just two, one will find some American theorists arguing that public education ought to instil the virtues essential for a democracy to flourish (Macedo, 1990) or those needed for cosmopolitan citizenship (Nussbaum, 2010).[4] Here, there is an essential reference to others besides the individual student; she is supposed to acquire the knowledge and skills needed to promote and participate in just power relations.

However, for one, it is implausible to think that these should be the sole or even primary final ends of education; they are best construed as supplementing other final ends. For another, as should become clear below, these relational elements are thin compared to other, non-Western traditions such as the African, where values of sociality are much richer and deemed essential to exhibit in many spheres of one's life, not just the political. For a third, these relational positions are rare in comparison with the intrinsic ones, which point also applies to the care-oriented thought about education of Nel Noddings (1984, 1992).

Turning now to the characteristic means by which final ends have been pursued in the West, consider that a large majority of it has (a) taken place in a dedicated school building and (b) been run by professional instructors in the light of (c) a preset, vetted curriculum that (d) has focused on written texts. In addition, the instruction (e) has sought to impart mainly propositional knowledge that categorises things and happenings and seeks underlying principles by which to account for them (f) established through argumentation, with students (g) oriented towards obtaining a degree or certificate so as to compete on a labour market and (h) being assessed on how well they each do on tests.[5]

Most of these elements are plausibly characterised as 'individualist' in some way, at least in comparison with education models salient in other parts of the world or in different eras. The (a) condition, about where the education takes place, is itself noteworthy for being separated from the broader community and the worlds of work, home and civil society. In addition, consider how the (b) and (c) elements keep students apart from each other and from the instructor; teachers are typically in control of a classroom such that most of the communication is unidirectional, coming 'downward' from a single source, and what they convey is unchanging in response to student particularity. As for (d), recall Marshall McLuhan's insightful reflections on the written word, and what new, isolating behaviours and interiorized mindsets came in the wake of reading books. The content of the books and other instruction (e) is typically focused not on developing interpersonal skills or understanding facets of the world in relational or holistic terms; it instead concentrates on classifying objects and events held to be able to known in isolation from other conditions (for which, see Nisbett, 2003). The technique by which such information is conveyed or supported is often a matter of argumentation (f), that is competition between competing hypotheses in which one seeks to win by virtue of marshalling the strongest evidence. Students are typically motivated by self-regarding considerations such as doing well on a competitive labour market, viz. obtaining a job and earning money (g). Finally, assessment is normally done so that each student is evaluated on her own (h).

Of course, there are exceptions to the above. However, I submit that it is the dominant approach to pedagogy in high schools and universities in Western countries and other societies heavily influenced by them. Since the above ends and means are salient in the West, that is have been recurrent there for a long while in a way they have not been elsewhere, at least not to the same degree, I dub them 'Western', in accordance with the previous account of how to use geographical labels.

I now consider which educational ends and means may be plausibly labelled 'African' or, more specifically, 'sub-Saharan', by virtue of being salient below the Sahara desert. With respect to final ends, it is well known that pre-colonial, and more generally indigenous, African education has mainly sought to enable students to undertake labour of a sort that would support their society, to impart the customs of the community to students, and to develop their moral excellence, understood as centred on a disposition to relate communally with others (Adeyemi & Adeyinka, 2003; Adeyinka & Ndwapi, 2002). Even contemporary discussions among sub-Saharan philosophers and thinkers about higher education have similarly focused substantially on the final ends of promoting development for the society as a whole, supporting local culture, and promoting moral personhood, or so I have discovered upon making a critical survey of more than 65 post-war texts in African higher education theory (Metz, 2009a).[6]

The relational or social dimensions of these goals are palpable, in comparison with those of the Western tradition. The interests or capacities of a given individual student considered in herself count for relatively little in the frameworks typical of sub-Saharan Africa; she is instead in the first instance directed outward, towards the interests of others or the flourishing of the group. The point of education is to enable her to take up work that would be of use to her society, to learn and adapt to its folkways, and to become the sort of person who treats others in a morally sound manner.

Note that I have been unable to find a single African thinker who extols the desirability of knowledge for its own sake. When this approach to intellectual engagement is discussed by sub-Saharans, they are invariably dismissive of it as inappropriate for an African context (for citations and discussion, see Metz, 2009b). In addition, whereas debate rages among Western theorists about whether moral education is permissible as a final end of at least higher education (see, for example, the contributions to Kiss & Euben, 2010), African ones by and large take it for granted as an appropriate goal.

With respect to means, sub-Saharans have also been less individualistic, and one might say extremely so when it comes to traditional practices among rural, small-scale societies. Returning to the schema that I used above, education (a★) was often undertaken in the community and 'on the job' and (b★) imparted by those with a particular 'know-how' or 'knowledge that' but no special training in pedagogical techniques in the light of (c★) a given student's gender and talents without review by some group of parents or officials and (d★) transmitted orally. In addition, the instruction (e★) sought to impart practical skills and parochial world views (f★) through rote memorization, imitation and group discussion, with students (g★) aiming to contribute to the well-being of their extended families and society more generally and (h★) not being formally assessed as individuals through tests scheduled at particular times, but rather by demonstrating an eventual acquisition of the skill or exhibiting an understanding in the course of collective dialogue.

Of course, contemporary education in urban environments below the Sahara hardly conforms to this 'ideal-type' (in the words of Weber) that was common before the influence of European settlers. However, one continues to find African education theorists advocating the adoption of means reminiscent of elements of this traditional orientation. For instance, one education theorist from South Africa contends that mathematics and science should include the learner's context and be 'embedded in the cultural practices of the African majority', for example by reflecting systematically on the fractal patterns of African traditional settlements (Seepe, 2000, pp. 131–133), while another similarly advocates local and participatory, or 'community-based', research (Nkomo, 2000, p. 53). For another example, a philosopher from Nigeria has argued in a systematic way for the view that certain types of 'indoctrination', and other forms of teaching that do not necessarily encourage student questioning, are appropriate as ways to impart virtue (Ikuenobe, 2006). Finally, Kwasi Wiredu, probably the most influential African philosopher alive, has contended that 'if education is an apprenticeship in the living of life in the community, then dialogue would naturally be one of its watchwords' (2004, p. 21), and I have similarly argued that an interest in realising communal relationships, central to characteristic African understandings of virtue and justice, recommends the creation of dialogical 'communities of educational practice' and the adoption of work-based learning (Metz, 2012).

My own view is that because of the salience of individualist ends and means in educational thought and practice in the West over many lifetimes, it is fair to think of 'Western' education as individualist, with similar remarks entailing that 'African' education counts as communitarian. To some readers, these labels will still seem overly restrictive and too exhaustive, objectionably implying that, for example, all and only educational elements in the West are individualist, which is of course not the case. Although the previous section makes clear, I believe, why it would be uncharitable to read the geographical labels in that way, perhaps such readers will at least accept that the Western is *more* individualist than the African, and, conversely, that the latter is *more* communitarian than the former. That will be enough to make my concluding point in the final section, that those in the West might have good reason to become less Western.

How to Question Individualism

I lack the space here to give adherents to characteristically Western positions about education a compelling rationale to change their mind. Instead, my aim is to indicate some prima facie reasons to doubt the attractiveness of the extent of individualism to be found in Euro-American thought and practice with respect to education, and to point out what it would mean for Westerners to change in a more communitarian direction.

Unfortunately, much of the so-called 'communitarian' criticism of liberalism and relatedly individualist trends in English-speaking philosophy of education and related theorization has not cut deeply. Too often, critics point out things to the effect that individuals cannot flourish on their own or that various institutions require certain kinds of social interaction in order to sustain themselves. However, these are sociological banalities, points that no one could reasonably question and that do not tell against individualism, construed in the first instance as an account of what to value as a final end. I am simply not aware of any influential Western thinker who has claimed that it is possible for, say, a child to grow up into a normal adult without socialisation or an adult to make substantial achievements as a Robinson Crusoe on a deserted island. Rebutting such empirical claims is, I submit, a waste of time that fails to move the debate forward; for even the most rabid egoist, individualist *par excellence*, will readily admit that in order for his self-interest to be maximised, he needs to rely on various kinds of positive sociality from family, friends, colleagues and neighbours. Hobbes hardly argued that one should live alone.

Where communitarian criticism has some bite is when it poses normative questions, about what makes a life worth living, how to treat others morally, or what public institutions ought to be striving to achieve, and when it posits essentially relational answers to them. Consider, for example, the idea that sometimes it is appropriate for people to make choices because 'this is who we are'. Note that one probably thinks at some level that loving and friendly relationships are to be valued for their own sake. Ponder the suggestion that a genuine psychopath, one utterly unable to empathise, to sympathise and to act for the sake of others, has a lower moral status than someone with these capacities. Think about the view that, when it comes to distributing goods in one's private capacity, one has basic moral reason to favour those for whom one cares and with whom one identifies. Reflect on the suggestion that one can have a duty to aid those related to one, but not because one has voluntarily assumed an obligation to do so by having promised. Notice the prima facie attractiveness of the idea that one function of a public school should be to overcome divisions of race, class and the like and to foster a sense of togetherness and that a government more generally ought to promote national cohesion in certain ways. Contemplate the notion that a public hospital should fund cosmetic surgery as necessary to facilitate romantic and other desirable social interaction. Pause over the perspective that one proper function of a criminal justice system should be to repair broken relationships between the offender and his direct and indirect victims. Finally, see that not to be dismissed is the idea that the state ought to support the institution of marriage (even if it should broaden its application in many jurisdictions) as well as to help fund counselling for couples and classes for parents.[7]

If one is sympathetic towards these kinds of approaches, then one will likely think that they should inform education and that the Western tradition needs correction to some degree. If one were to construct a philosophy of education that posited relational final ends, as well as means that gave independent weight to relational considerations, then one would in effect be developing a non-Western, or at least less Western, viewpoint. Given the current meaning of the word 'Western' and cognate terms, as referring to long-standing individualist thought and practice in Euro-America, a more communitarian approach on the part of those living there would *mean becoming not so Western.*

However, recall my point that what counts as 'Western', or what more generally falls under the heading of geographical labels, is not fixed. If there occurred a systematic shift among those living in the West towards communitarian world views and ways of life, then what the term 'Western' refers to would change. Over time, given enough movement away from individualism in Euro-American contexts, the Western would become communitarian. To return to the philosophy of language, although I do not believe that geographical labels are identical in function to indexicals such as 'you' and 'this',[8] they are similar in that their linguistic content varies, depending on the context in which they are used.

As someone who is sympathetic towards the communitarian normative perspectives adumbrated above, I conclude that the West should become less Western, or, in other words, that it ought to change what the meaning of 'Western' is. However, as someone who also believes that those in the African tradition often miss out on some kernels of truth in Euro-American viewpoints, particularly with regard to the value of knowledge for its own sake (Metz, 2009b, 2013), I am also partial to the idea that those in Africa should become less African. My hope is that this article has made the coherence, if not attractiveness, of such claims apparent to the reader.

Notes

1. And, furthermore, without suggesting that people in these locations are morally obligated to hold views with such features.
2. I here acknowledge the political sensitivities about the use of the term 'African' and cognate words. Some have argued that it is immoral or otherwise inappropriate to use such terms, given that they are apparently colonial conceptual impositions and not the way indigenous black peoples initially referred to themselves (e.g. Ramose, 2004, pp. 145–146).
3. Discussed by Nisbett (2003) in contrast to characteristically East Asian approaches to knowledge.
4. And for a recent collection of work that forms an alternative to analytic liberal approaches to the philosophy of education, see Carr (2005).
5. I borrow some of this schema from Metz (2012), but have enriched it here.
6. I note that a concern to rectify injustice has also figured prominently (e.g. Nkomo, 2000; Ramose, 2004), but I set it aside as a contingent and 'non-ideal' end, that is one that arises only in the context of serious wrongdoing at the societal level.

7. For discussion and defence of a number of these ideas, see Metz (2010) and Metz and Gaie (2010).
8. Whereas indexicals plausibly rigidly designate, referring to the essence of a being in all possible worlds (as per Kaplan, 1989), I doubt that geographical labels do and believe they instead pick out a collection of properties or, perhaps, a subject of such a collection.

References

Adeyemi, M., & Adeyinka, A. (2003). The principles and content of African traditional education. *Educational Philosophy and Theory, 35*, 425–440.

Adeyinka, A., & Ndwapi, G. (2002). Education and morality in Africa. *Pastoral Care in Education, 20*, 17–23.

Aristotle. (350 B.C.E.). *Nicomachean ethics*. (W. D. Ross, Trans.). Retrieved from http://classics.mit.edu/Aristotle/nicomachaen.html

Carr, W. (Ed.). (2005). *The RoutledgeFalmer reader in philosophy of education*. London: RoutledgeFalmer.

Horsthemke, K., & Enslin, P. (2005). Is there a distinctly and uniquely African philosophy of education? In Y. Waghid & B. Van Wyk (Eds.), *African(a) philosophy of education* (pp. 54–75). Stellenbosch: Department of Education Policy Studies, Stellenbosch University.

Husserl, E. (1935). *Philosophy and the crisis of European man*. (Q. Lauer, Trans.). Retrieved from www.users.cloud9.net/~bradmcc/husserl_philcris.html

Ikuenobe, P. (2006). *Philosophical perspectives on communalism and morality in African traditions*. Lanham, MD: Rowman & Littlefield.

Kaplan, D. (1989). Demonstratives. In J. Almog, J. Perry, & H. Wettstein (Eds.), *Themes from Kaplan* (pp. 481–563). Oxford: Oxford University Press.

Kiss, E., & Euben, J. P. (Eds.). (2010). *Debating moral education: Rethinking the role of the modern university*. Durham, NC: Duke University Press.

Macedo, S. (1990). *Liberal virtues*. New York, NY: Oxford University Press.

Metz, T. (2009a). The final ends of higher education in light of an African moral theory. *Journal of Philosophy of Education, 43*, 179–201.

Metz, T. (2009b). Higher education, knowledge for its own sake, and an African moral theory. *Studies in Philosophy and Education, 28*, 517–536.

Metz, T. (2010). For the sake of the friendship: Relationality and relationship as grounds of beneficence. *Theoria, 57*, 54–76.

Metz, T. (2012). Communitarian ethics and work-based education: Some African perspectives. In P. Gibbs (Ed.), *Learning, work and practice: New understandings* (pp. 191–206). Dordrecht: Springer.

Metz, T. (2013). A dilemma about the final ends of higher education–And a resolution. *Kagisano, 9*, 23–41.

Metz, T., & Gaie, J. (2010). The African ethic of ubuntu/botho: Implications for research on morality. *Journal of Moral Education, 39*, 273–290.

Nisbett, R. (2003). *The geography of thought: How Asians and Westerners think differently*. New York, NY: Simon & Schuster.

Nkomo, M. (2000). Educational research in the African development context. In P. Higgs, N. C. G. Vakalisa, T. V. Mda, & N. T. Assie-Lumumba (Eds.), *African voices in education* (pp. 47–62). Lansdowne: Juta & Co. Ltd.

Noddings, N. (1984). *Caring: A feminine approach to ethics and moral education*. Berkeley: University of California Press.

Noddings, N. (1992). *The challenge to care in schools*. New York, NY: Teachers College Press.

Nussbaum, M. (2010). *Not for profit: Why democracy needs the humanities*. Princeton: Princeton University Press.

Parker, B. (2003). Back on the chain gang: Some difficulties in developing a (South) African philosophy of education. *Journal of Education, 30*, 23–40.

Ramose, M. (2004). In search of an African philosophy of education. *South African Journal of Higher Education, 18*, 138–160.

Seepe, S. (2000). Africanization of knowledge. In P. Higgs, N. C. G. Vakalisa, T. V. Mda, & N. T. Assie-Lumumba (Eds.), *African voices in education* (pp. 118–138). Lansdowne: Juta & Co. Ltd.

Wiredu, K. (2004). Prolegomena to an African philosophy of education. *South African Journal of Higher Education, 18*, 17–26.

Human Freedom and the Philosophical Attitude

SHARON RIDER
Department of Philosophy, Uppsala University

Abstract

Attempts to describe the essential features of the Western philosophical tradition can often be characterized as 'boundary work', that is, the attempt to create, promote, attack, or reinforce specific notions of the 'philosophical' in order to demarcate it as a field of intellectual inquiry. During the last century, the dominant tendency has been to delineate the discipline in terms of formal methods, techniques, and concepts and a given set of standard problems and alternative available solutions (although this element has been both present and at times highly influential at least since Plato). One vital feature of the philosophical tradition that has played a certain rather subterranean but nonetheless indispensable role, which I will discuss in this article, is that of repeatedly and stringently calling into question the conditions of its own possibility. The Cartesian tradition (including Kant, Husserl, Popper and Weber) shares with the anti-philosophers (say, Nietzsche and Kierkegaard, but even the later Wittgenstein) the insight that this questioning itself is and has always been a problem, perhaps the deepest problem, for philosophy. The idea that one has the right, even the responsibility, to pose questions that are non-standard, not comme il faut, perhaps even taboo, lay at the very heart of notions such as 'the pursuit of truth', 'vita contemplativa', and 'philosophy as work on oneself'. On what grounds can one possibly assert such a right? In the Western tradition, it has most often been associated with a form of genuine doubt founded in deep engagement with some subject matter, i.e. the notion that one has a 'problem' demanding that one take responsibility for one's beliefs and thoughts, both morally and logically. It seems to me that the meaning of this most basic attitude is something that each generation must rediscover for itself; indeed, recreate for itself in a new environment and under new conditions. Thus, the blindness of the past, in this self-understanding of philosophy, need not bind or blind us in the future. To the contrary, the European intellectual tradition can be seen as providing a series of perspicuous representations of intermittently faltering and flourishing attempts at asserting the viability of the idea of human freedom as essentially bound up with the pursuit of truth. As such, it is of necessity open to perpetual revision (even when it resists it).

THE DILEMMA OF WESTERN PHILOSOPHY

1. Two Understandings of the Discipline of Philosophy

There are today two distinct but related challenges to the continuation of the discipline known as 'philosophy'. In the end, they are one, but seen from two perspectives: the challenge from within and the challenge from without. Starting with the latter, the very organizational prerequisites and their attendant professional perquisites have been radically called into question. The response from academic philosophy has been to address problems such as diminishing student enrollments and skeptical university managers by applying 'philosophical methods' to the interests and worries of the day and developing programs of study and research projects in which these can be integrated. Such initiatives to provide economic opportunities for departments and contribute to improving general education in other fields have, of course, existed for decades in the form of courses in ethics for students in business and medicine (business ethics, biomedical ethics). And, given the organizational and economic structure of universities, it was only natural that research programs and projects should follow. In other areas of philosophy, such as formal logic and to some extent the philosophy of science, the pattern was somewhat different. These are fields in which questions arising out of conceptual problems internal to scientific practice resulted in specific methods and theories that could then be taught and studied as 'specializations'. Cognitive science is an example of a field where philosophical theorizing could be put to practical use in this way. In the last few decades, we have seen an explosion in attempts to put philosophy to work at something concrete or, as one might say, to give it a job description. There are now a plethora of work packages for ethicists: the 'classics' mentioned earlier (biomedical ethics and business ethics), as well as environmental ethics, research ethics, population ethics, and digital ethics, to name a few. Alternatively, there are courses of study and programs of research in decision theory for organizations, risk management for sustainable urban planning, etc. In short, the move is toward making philosophy 'relevant' to real life and the real world. This move presupposes, of course, that in and of itself, philosophy is *not* relevant. In my view, this pervasive assumption poses a much more profound menace to philosophy, both as an academic discipline and, more critically, as a possible form of human thought.

The relevance or irrelevance of philosophy as such is not self-evident. It depends entirely on what conception of philosophy is at stake. In one conception, namely, the dominant one, philosophy is a special science that has progressed to achieve a relatively high degree of precision, due in no small part to formalization. Intrinsic to this precision and the reliability of the results emanating from it is sub-specialization within the field. An expert in value theory is no more an expert in the philosophy of mathematics than an astrophysicist is expert in climatology. In both cases, there are surely certain very basic notions in common, but they are not of the kind apposite for dealing adequately with particular advanced problems within the field. Each area of specialization has its own methods and modus operandi, and while there may be greater or lesser degree of overlap between fields, proficiency in a given field requires mastery of the concepts, techniques and operations germane to the area of specialization in question. On this conception of philosophy, the question of relevance is conceived in the same way as in any science: one distinguishes between 'basic', 'pure' or 'fundamental' research, on the one hand, and 'applied research', on the other. As in the natural sciences, the distinction is not absolute, but rather a question of to what degree the research involved is formulated so as to solve a problem not issuing out of scientific inquiry itself, but posed as a practical problem by some external agent, authority, or interest. Metaphysics and epistemology, as a rule, fall on the far side of 'pure research', while digital ethics are substantially practical in their orientation. Even within a particular branch, however, there is a spectrum between theoretical and applied orientations. In the philosophy of law, for example, basic questions regarding the nature of laws and rights are among the most abstract and fundamental, whereas applied legal philosophy attends to particular aspects of the law in relation to the social and political context of legislation and reform. And once again, even here, there is room for work stressing the theoretical framework, which would be more 'basic' than one analyzing a specific piece of jurisprudence against a socio-political backdrop by utilizing some philosophical theory.

This conception of philosophy follows the pattern of science generally, then, in accepting that scientific advancement presupposes specialization. But also, as in science generally, there is a kind of 'remainder' left every time a border is drawn between areas of inquiry and their methods and theories that justifies asking more fundamental questions about the possibilities and limits of those methods and theories. The notion of 'pure research' is just the notion that a certain degree of intellectual autonomy is part and parcel of the pursuit of scientific truth. It is the freedom to ask ourselves what we are doing, why we are doing it, and if we might not be doing something wrong or if we could or should do something else.

When such questions arise, one natural first step is to retrace our steps, as it were, and try to understand how it came about that we started thinking in this way, i.e. to reflect historically on the presuppositions or conditioning intellectual context that made possible a certain way of thinking. 'Historical reflection' here need not be understood in terms of intellectual history, although such considerations are often highly pertinent, even inevitable, for understanding the development of a certain kind of discourse. But historical reflection can be understood more broadly, as questions in this borderland between or beyond academic disciplines that ask precisely what is it that we are doing *now*. Foucault's idea that Kant's essays on the Enlightenment and the French Revolution introduced a new question into philosophy, namely, the question of the contemporaneity of the now, makes a similar point. In science, we are agents in a self-contained activity that has certain predetermined rules of play. But in posing the question, 'what is happening?' we are both agent and element. The question forces on the one who poses it a state of intellectual self-reflection and reflexivity, and thus, neutralizes any and all 'natural' categories, concepts, distinctions, practices, routines, and techniques. (Foucault, 1986, pp. 88–96). This kind of reflection does not properly belong to science, since, rather than taking for granted the conceptual framework and methods that constitute a discipline and the kinds of objects it studies, it interrogates these concepts and models as objects of autonomous scrutiny, that is, unbiased and unconstrained analytical examination and evaluation. On this point, there is not serious disagreement between, say, Kuhn and Popper. The difference is that Kuhn would say that this sort of discussion without a unitary paradigm is outside science properly speaking, while Popper considers it an ever present possibility belonging intrinsically to the very idea of science, properly understood. In either case, this idea of the freedom and hope of science share important characteristics with an altogether different conception of philosophy than as that of a special science.

If philosophy is not a science in its own right, what can it be? The most common alternative to the idea of philosophy as a science is that of philosophy as a special genre of scholarly commentary. In this paradigm, philosophy consists in the appropriation, contemplation, and explication of its own history. The value or relevance of studying thinkers of the past is often associated, among other things, with Bildung, or with the importance of historical perspective. Often, although certainly not always, there exists an implicit form of historical realism that motivates the study, an idea that there is a singular correct way of understanding what, say, Kant had on his mind and wanted others to understand, and that this correct interpretation is at one with the most highly regarded and widely accepted scholarly commentaries. But this idea can and often does lead to an emphasis on the text as a presentation or product, that is, as a system or structure of theses and doctrines, rather than as someone's actual living thoughts, that is, as a way of thinking. It can also lead to a tendency to use the text in question to confirm or reinforce contemporary conceptions of a set of ideas associated with the name of Kant, for instance, which in turn is used to confirm or reinforce contemporary dominant conceptions more generally, in science, scholarship, or politics. When these conceptions are altered, the manner of reading Kant, 'what he said', is altered with it. In short, the history of philosophy as a scholarly discipline is concerned with placing and positioning texts deemed 'philosophical' within the academic community in a certain historical representational context. But this academic activity, as a discipline, has its own canon of exemplary texts, scholarly standards, standard techniques, and accepted solutions. In this respect, philosophy as commentary and interpretation, that is, as scholarship, follows the same pattern of philosophy understood as a science.

Foucault's suggestion above does not belong to this tradition. Rather, it follows Kant in that the attitude that Foucault takes toward his object here is non-dogmatic (in the Kantian sense) with regard to Kant exegesis, commentary, and interpretation. Rather than justify or reaffirm, his approach is rather tentative and comparative. His technique does not aim to provide a 'true' or 'correct' interpretation of Kant, but to read Kant in such a way as to loosen the grip of constrained readings, namely, those that come 'naturally' due to our contemporary notions and ways of thinking. In this respect, the object is not the Enlightenment, but the present. The aim is actually double: to see what ideas and notions that we find in Kant that are still relevant and valid (that is to say, useful), and just how relevant and valid they are; and to see which are obsolete and invalid (that is to say, not useful), so that we can leave them behind as historical artifacts not belonging to our way of life. The difference between this 'method' of philosophical thought and standard scholarship in the history of philosophy can be described in terms of the perspective taken on the thoughts considered. The scholarly approach within the history of philosophy as an academic discipline is to study Kant's philosophy in terms of the doctrines for which it became famous: the *results* of his thinking; what he said and how he said it. Indeed, Kant left us with a philosophical vocabulary that we can barely do without, its influence on later philosophy comparable with that of the King James bible or Shakespeare's tragedies on the development of modern English.

But there is again here what was termed earlier a 'remainder', what is beyond the ideas, doctrines, theories, positions, standpoints, and various 'isms'. It's doubtful that the uncontested canonical philosophers (Plato, Aristotle, Descartes, Hume, Kant) saw their life's work as consisting of a contest between established doctrines. Kant explicitly denies that he is concerned with hypotheses and standpoints at all (cf. Kant, 1965, A xv–xvi and B xxxv–xxxvii). Kant also denies that the understanding of a work in philosophy that approaches it as a system of doctrines is a philosophical understanding (Kant, 1965, A 484/B 512).

An alternative conception of philosophy is to see it as constituted by problems—not in the sense of intellectual puzzles, but in the sense of deep concerns requiring great intellectual exertion. Theories and theses are, in this view, merely instruments or means by which to solve a problem. Thus, it makes no sense to treat theories and theses as external to or disconnected from the problem at hand. Plato's diaeresis, Kant's critical philosophy, Hegel's dialectic, Freud's psychoanalysis, or Foucault's genealogical method are all responses to a certain kind of question, and the value and even to a great extent the sense of those answers are indistinguishable from how the question is formulated and what it means. With regard to older texts, this means that the intellectual historical environment in which the problem(s) and their attendant theories, theses, and concepts were used and the language in which they were formulated are unavoidably part of the understanding of the problem. Or, as Collingwood famously put it, 'we only know what the problem was by arguing back from the solution' (Collingwood, 2002, p. 70). Our own ideas, concepts, and vocabulary are as historically determined as those in the works that we study. In this understanding of philosophy, this insight is fundamental for philosophy, while it is for the most part irrelevant for the special sciences. Past and present intellectual traditions are mutually dependent insofar as both are affected by how Kant, for example, is and has been read. Our contemporary ways of dealing with the philosophical problems that troubled Kant are an expression and result of that historical conceptual formation. The developments and connections are not transparent for the reasons cited in connection with Foucault above: in thinking through the problems, we are at once agents and elements of the concept formation that is the precondition of our own thinking. The natural starting point for all thinking is to take our own starting points as self-evident and necessary without regard to the choices and decisions that were made at some point, which lead to that just these concepts and solutions and not others came to be taken for granted as given, obvious and indispensable.[1]

If one thing has become clear, it is that current ideas about what constitutes an academic discipline are under pressure from all corners, and are neither obvious nor regarded as necessary. But in considering the future and the present of the discipline of philosophy, it can be helpful to consider the relation between two senses of 'discipline': on the one hand, a field of study, branch of knowledge, subject area, field of specialization or systematic instruction, and so forth, and, on the other, the idea of control or self-control that the former assumes. The notion of discipline in the first sense can be described as the training of a disciple, that is, the expectations placed on someone engaged in a craft or order with a set of norms or a code of conduct to which he has committed himself. But it can also be described from the perspective of the disciple himself, in terms of the self-control or self-mastery he aims to achieve by submitting himself to the exercises and system of reward and punishment of the institution. A disciple's highest goal is to achieve the continence of the master, that is, his ability perform consistently well because his aims and desires conform to his knowledge and reason. This sense of the 'discipline' of philosophy echoes in part Hadot's Wittgensteinian idea that the activity of philosophy at its inception was characterized by 'spiritual exercises', i.e. 'practices ... intended to effect a modification and a transformation in the subjects who practice them' (Hadot, 2002). On this 'therapeutic' view, contemporary philosophy as an academic discipline understanding itself as a special science is a misunderstanding and distortion of the basic idea of philosophy, which is concerned with the True, the Just, and the Good, not as theoretical abstractions, but a way of life. Theorizing is a means (among others), not an end in itself.

2. Transcendental Philosophy as an Exercise in Freedom and Discipline

In *Discipline and Punish* and elsewhere, Foucault makes the argument that '(t)he disciplines characterize, classify, specialize; they distribute along a scale, around a norm, hierarchize individuals in relation to one another and, if necessary, disqualify and invalidate' (Foucault, 1979, p. 223). Educational disciplines as we know them, that is, as describing institutional boundaries, came rather late on the scene, largely the final result of late eighteenth- and early nineteenth-century attempts to catalog and control the rapidly growing body of scientific results and culminating in the American system of departmental organization (Clarke, 2007). Our 'traditional' divisions into 'the natural sciences' of physics, chemistry, biology, geology, and astronomy, 'the social science disciplines' of economics, politics, sociology, and psychology, and 'the humanistic studies' of languages, philosophy, history, and literature are relatively recent conventions. Prior to the nineteenth century, what we call 'scientists' were known as Natural Historians (life sciences) and Natural Philosophers (physics), and they were amateurs associated mostly with academies rather than universities. In any case, modern scientific specialization developed in tandem with the departmentalization of teaching and the university, which increasingly became the main financial source and institutional structure of scientific activity. With specialization, there emerged ever more concentrated areas of expertise, manifested most notably in the advent of specialized journals. Further, academic disciplines are intimately linked to the evolution of professions, since it is the disciplinary field that determines and authorizes the necessary and sufficient knowledge for admission into the profession and the criteria by which proficiency and expertise are assessed. One might say that academic disciplines are in the business of keeping thought in line, of keeping it in its place through the socialization and thus self-regulation of its practitioners, as it were. It is intrinsically a matter of community standards, criteria, and norms. Philosophy as understood in the alternative understanding sketched above, on the other hand, arises out of doubt or intellectual dissatisfaction, a sense that something is missing or not quite right in accepted theories and habit of thought that belong to them. The freedom of philosophy, in this conception, is the act of taking ones doubts seriously, claiming the right to hesitate before acceding to convention or contemporary manner and mores, and reflecting upon the basis for one's own assumptions and intellectual inclinations.

Another word for this reluctance is 'second thoughts', or, one might say, a more thoughtful kind of *thinking*. At the same time, the hesitation presupposes that there is or may be some truth or idea or insight that one hopes or suspects can be found that guides the direction of one's thoughts. To maintain direction, to find what one is seeking, requires self-discipline and self-determination, since there is no external authority to serve as the given touchstone which will give the seeker satisfaction except his own sense that he has come to clarity. A certain idea of freedom as intrinsic to the philosophical enterprise is as ancient as it is modern, namely, the idea of self-legislation or autonomy. This idea is not coterminous with liberty. The latter is broad enough to encompass an idea of boundless and facile freedom, while the exercise of autonomy requires an enormous effort on the part of the individual. One possible idea of freedom in the sense of liberty is the freedom to do whatever one pleases, to follow one's inclinations without hindrance. (Indeed, some of the critique of modern liberal democracy today stems from dissatisfaction with the limits it places on the possibility of fulfilling wishes and desires. Legislation criminalizing non-consensual intercourse even between spouses or corporal punishment of one's own children as impingements of freedom within the private sphere would be a case in point.) Self-legislation, on the other hand, is the idea that one can learn to observe, understand, and even modify, that is, master, one's wishes and desires. Autonomy as an ideal then is freedom from both external constraints and internal compulsions, including those beliefs and attitudes that seem to come so naturally that one barely recognizes that they exist.

What kind of an idea is this? Robert Pippin asks:

> what is the real content of this ideal (what would it be to lead a free life) and why has it become so important to us, what is its importance to us—are obviously pretty vague, it already does not look like a strictly philosophical answer to those questions could get us very far, at least it doesn't seem likely to me. It is after all only relatively recently in Western history that we began to think of human beings as something like individuals directing and guiding the course of their own lives, in some sense independent and self-determining centers of a causal agency; only relatively recently that one's entitlement to such a self-determining, self-directed life seemed not just valuable but absolutely valuable, for the most part more important even than any consideration of security, well-being, and peace that would make the attainment of such an ideal more difficult, so important that it was even worth the risk of life in its defense. (Pippin, 2006, p. 87)

And, in partial response to his own question concerning how the ideal of autonomy came to take hold of the western imagination, he notes that even if we concede to all historicizing accounts describing the *de facto* conditions of this development, often aimed at demonstrating the contingency of those conditions, we have not satisfied the impulse to ask questions concerning the normative status of the ideal. And those questions are acute. He continues:

> At just the moment in the nineteenth century when Western European societies, for all of their visible flaws, seemed to start paying off the Enlightenment's promissory notes, reducing human misery by the application of their new science and technology, increasing the authority of appeals to reason in life, reducing the divisive public role of religion, extending the revolutionary claim of individual natural right to an ever wider class of subjects, accelerating the extension of natural scientific explanation, and more and more actually gaining what Descartes so boldly promised, the mastery of nature, it also seemed that many of the best, most creative minds produced within and as products of such societies rose up in protest, even despair at the social organization and norms that also made all of this possible. In painting, literature, and music, as well as philosophy, bourgeois modernity as a whole became not only a great problem but also a very confusing, largely distasteful fate. All this eventually came to be reflected in what the profession classifies as continental philosophy—the end of metaphysics, the end of philosophy, the impotence of reason, failed signifiers, the death of the subject, the end of man, negative dialectics, the impossibility of poetry, the end of the novel, absolute contingency, anti-humanism, and on and on. (Pippin, 2006, p. 89)

If one wants to see what might still be useful, veridical, or relevant in this idea today, one way of going about it is to try to understand it in terms of what it meant for philosophy when it came to be articulated, again, not as an intra-theoretical problem belonging to one set of specialized questions (moral philosophy or ethics or political philosophy) but as a way of thinking about real problems, where the divisions between theoretical and practical, or between different disciplines, are not assumed beforehand.

In what follows, we will return to the example of Kant. Kant will be used here not as an object of scholarly interpretation, but as an illustration of two things: first, as an example of a different conception of philosophy than that of a special science, and second, as an example of how one might approach the philosophical tradition without reducing it to a canon of doctrines, on the one hand, or mere white mythology or rationalized pietism, etc. on the other. The approach is to try to follow Kant's train of thought as emanating from a real need or desire, to read back to the question, as Collingwood would say, to understand what one must take oneself to be doing in order to invent Kantian critical philosophy and the doctrines and distinctions associated with it. On this way of reading Kant, the doctrines and distinctions, that is, the products or results of his thinking, regarded solely as products or results, are in and of themselves no different from the products of any earlier or competing systems. What is distinct for Kant's critical philosophy is its *method*, which he thinks guarantees the validity of the results. And it is the validity or truthfulness that is the aim of philosophy as described above. The critical method, in contrast to dogmatic philosophy, is characterized by autonomy. While dogmatic thinking does not and cannot question its own resources, conditions, and procedures, the critical method subjects itself to strenuous self-critique. While dogmatic thinking assumes the sense and applicability of certain basic concepts and distinctions as unquestionable and non-negotiable (to the extent it even recognizes that they are in play), that its procedures and applications are reliable and sound (to the extent that it even recognizes that it is following predetermined procedures), and takes the results of those assumptions consequently as demonstrated truths, critical philosophy places the object of inquiry in relation to the grounds or assumptions in which the question is framed, and asks if those grounds are sufficient for an adequate answer, and if so, how it is possible (Kant, 1965, A 484/B 512). On this view, philosophy is the conviction that is possible to separate truth from error, in the first instance, in one's own thinking. Kant does not claim to prove that the conclusions arrived at by means of his method are true, merely to have shown that it is possible. And that possibility is what entitles us to try, since it does not violence to reason to attempt the possible.

Kant is an interesting example for our purposes in part because he thematizes one of the central issues of this article, namely, the autonomy of philosophy with respect to the special sciences. The idea that it is possible and necessary (even urgent, if we share the concerns of later thinkers in the Kantian tradition such as Husserl) to systematically articulate the absolute unconditional principles for all knowledge is one that has lost salience in philosophy. But for Kant and his contemporaries, the conditions, possibilities, and limitations of the paradigmatic forms of *Wissenschaft*, that is, mathematics and the physical sciences, were of foremost concern. Kant's hesitation regarding the scientific status of metaphysics as it had hitherto been conducted, i.e. his suspicion that metaphysics was not a science at all, was the starting point of the *Critique of Pure Reason*. The problem he found was not primarily with the results (doctrines, claims, and teachings) of metaphysics, but with its methods. The methods appropriate to the special sciences, and which serve them well, lead irrevocably to the formulation of basic problems that of necessity result not in justified true knowledge, but in antinomies of reason. The sciences are defined and delimited by the methods employed to solve distinct and determinate problems. Such methodological predetermined delimitation is useless and potentially harmful to a form of inquiry lacking that kind of object. What remains for philosophical inquiry that hopes to have the rigor and epistemic accountability of the special sciences is to direct its attentions to its own resources, possibilities, and delimitations, that is, to take itself as its own object. Thus, metaphysics is possible precisely as thinking about the conditions of thought, or reason's critique of itself; as Kant puts it, in philosophical reflection 'reason is occupied with nothing but itself' (Kant, 1965, A 680/B 708). Kant's discussion of the antinomies attempts to show how metaphysical problems dissolve as real questions (that is, as questions about 'reality') when they are understood as questions concerning our own faculties, the resources we have at our disposal, for construing and answering the kinds of questions that we are inclined to pose.[2] Principles, concepts, and categories that belong to our ways of dealing with empirical matters cannot simply be shifted to an entirely other kind of question without loss of meaning and with it coherence. If the legitimate use of the language and categories of empirical knowledge is limited to matters concerning possible empirical experience, then the aim of the critique of reason is to investigate the foundations of empirical and mathematical claims to knowledge with regard to its conditions and resources. In his forward to the *Critique of Pure Reason*, Kant says that his point in not simply to reject certain kinds of problems as belonging properly to science due to the limitations of the human intellect. To the contrary, Kant is deeply impressed by the enormous power of science and the breadth of its results. But he wants to know how the knowledge that science produces is possible, and he recognizes that the question of the possibility of science is not a question belonging to any of the special sciences. By the same token, he is not as impressed with the results of 2000 years of metaphysics, and he asks himself how it is possible to formulate problems in such a way that it is immune to a straightforward and unequivocal answer.

When Kant asks how the sciences are possible, he does not begin with the given facts, methods, and concepts as they are used in the sciences but with the question of in what such knowledge can be grounded, what sort of foundations would have to hold for the results to be true and valid. This question, the question of a priori conditions, is the question of the possibilities and limitations of the idea of knowledge, and it leads to a transcendental thinking, a thinking in which knowledge is related to what is known, the thought.[3] The sciences ask for the objective grounds for a judgment, while transcendental philosophy asks what it means for a thinking subject to make or grasp such a judgment to begin with. But in a transcendental reflection (that is, in critical philosophy), the subject is not in the first instance to be understood empirically or psychologically, but *a priori*. The 'I' in question is an ideal 'I', an 'I' in the bare-bones sense of the logical subject of thinking, apart from its particularity and contingent characteristics. Precisely this aspect of Kantian philosophy is regarded today with suspicion in many quarters, as at best a quaint remnant of old, European metaphysics that we do not have to take very seriously. But this response is rather exaggerated, and blinds us to what sense we can make of it, and what value it might have for our own thinking. In a great deal of everyday discourse, we often make reference to phenomena in an attitude of non-situated impersonal knowledge. When we talk about plants and animals, we do it as a rule in a way that is not conceptually bound with our own 'private' experiences. We quite simply mean different things by these terms, regardless of our ethnicity, gender, social or economic conditions, or personal history of tulips and aardvarks. Now of course prior knowledge of etiology or horticulture, various cultural associations with certain kinds of flowers, dietary laws, etc. will likely inform when, where, and how the distinction comes into play, but that very observation assumes that we already understand what we are talking about in the first place. In this sense, we share a common form of life, even if that commonality may mislead us into assuming a false universality or even necessity to more local, contingent, or specific variations than is warranted.

It will be recalled that 'transcendental idealism' does not contradict empirical realism; it takes it as its starting point (Kant, 1965, A 367–380). Rather than denying the reality of the external world, Kant takes for granted that we have experience of aardvarks and tulips. But what he hopes to achieve by means of his critical method is to provide an answer to the question, 'given that I experience x as x, how is it possible? What conditions must hold?' And this question is not posed from an external point of view in the manner of Hume, as a question concerning some empirical object (the psychological subject or I), but from the point of view of the experience itself. A transcendental investigation concerns the sense of the concepts necessarily involved in discrete experience (this is the point of Kant's remark that intuitions without concepts are blind). What characterizes transcendental reflection is that it does not result in 'valid knowledge' about some (empirical) thing, since it does not concern things in the world. Outside of the reflection, it has no sense at all. When Kant points out that concepts without intuitions are empty, and intuitions without concepts are blind, he is not making an empirical claim about the relation between two things. He is saying that in any case of the phenomenon of Y, for it to be Y, it must be recognizable as such. Otherwise there would be no phenomenon, since to be a phenomenon is to be apprehended. But Y, the form itself, is a function of thinking, and the distinction between thinking and apprehending can only be thought, not perceived. It is not something that we can arrive at through experience. But such a statement is not part of knowledge of or about the world; it is not part of science and it is not ontology (or rather, ontology, for Kant, is only possible as epistemology). His question is not 'What are phenomena and how are they related to consciousness', but rather 'How are we to philosophize so as to better understand the nature, applicability and limitations of empirical knowledge?' One might even consider the entirety of his philosophy in light of the desire to answer that question. But if it is right and reasonable to say that his answers cannot help us due to historical developments in science and society, as well as in logic, mathematics, and philosophy, it is not at all clear that it is uninteresting and unhelpful to pose similar questions about *our* science, *our* logic, and *our* philosophy. To the contrary, one might think that the question has never been more relevant or the need for a viable answer more pressing.

We can 'situate' Kantian thinking in a narrative about Western European thinking and its bourgeois assumptions in which a certain form of white, male heteronormative rationality is reified and fetishized, but then we have not even begun to raise the question of the normative validity of the ideal whatever its origin. But not asking the question is not the same thing as having answered it. It is not really clear that we have even fully understood what this account of philosophy is, or what potential applicability it has. One of the more salient aspects of his philosophy is Kant's delimitation of the valid domain of scientific authority, one that is far from what we should rightly call 'positivist'. Kant quite explicitly rejects the sovereignty of the sciences over human existence. Science or scientific thinking is the name for a human activity; it is something we do to satisfy certain needs, including the need to find answers to the questions and doubts that arise in our experience. One of his main concerns in accounting for the conditions for possible experience is to show that certain problems are not amenable to scientific proof, since they are not objects of experience and therefore cannot be objects of scientific proof (the ideas of God, the soul and the cosmos). Equally important for Kant is to show that this limitation need not lead to skepticism; to the contrary what appears to be a limitation is in fact not a real limitation at all, but appears to be one if we make the sort of conceptual mistake described above, namely, that of taking transcendental questions as substantial ones, with objective empirical (i.e. substantial) answers. At the same time, Kant says that the 'limitation' of scientific knowledge, the boundaries of what can be said substantially, is not a limitation at all, but rather a demonstration of our freedom. We are free to hesitate when we encounter metaphysical and dogmatic claims about freedom and necessity, and free to rely on our own reason rather than external authority in the form of 'established truths' and ask ourselves if these arguments actually bring us closer to satisfying answers to questions that are of the greatest concern for us. For questions regarding Nature and limits of the human capacity to attain to the truth, to understand the world around us and our place in it, questions concerning the freedom of the will and the order of nature, are always relevant and always momentous, at least for some. But the answers that have been offered have not satisfied our need to know what is the case precisely because they treat nature and the will as kinds of objects, as possible objects of knowledge. According to Kant, they are not and cannot be. They are *ideas of reason,* not concepts of the understanding. And ideas of this kind make it meaningful to continue thinking and trying to act rightly and justly, because we are human beings who choose and not machines that merely process information, blindly and dumbly following the rules of understanding. It is nonsense to speak of truth or validity with regard to such ideas. They are regulative; they constitute the very condition of our humanity. Kant saw clearly that if would be difficult for us to 'take the transcendental turn' in our thinking. Our reason must learn to tame, to discipline, the very desires that motivate and justify its use. But there is a clear difference between bridling desire and satisfying needs. On that point, however, Kant was not an idealist but a realist, in the popular sense, in the end, the choice is not ours. Our autonomy consists in nothing but our capacity to recognize and follow the dictates that we legislate for ourselves out of our reason, to listen to reason, one might say, since we are at heart rational beings. In that respect, it is probably fair to say that not only Kant, but the intellectual tradition for which he might well be said to be the foremost representative, is a relic of a past form of life. Were it otherwise, if we really could make use of Kant as he intended, then philosophy would be alive and well and in no need of further justification.

Funding

This work was supported by the Swedish Research Council [grant number 721-2013-2317].

Notes

1. Consider, for instance, certain concepts that were derived from Kant's thought (Kant's particular way of formulating the distinctions between subject and object, *a priori* and a posteriori, analytic and synthetic, empirical and logical, as well as the very ideas of 'intuition', 'evidence', etc. in philosophy), but due to certain historical developments in philosophy and logic came to be used in different ways. When Frege posed the question of whether mathematical propositions are synthetic, it wasn't the same question as Kant's, in part because they didn't have the same conception of arithmetic. Kant wanted to deduce mathematics from our apprehension of time. For Frege, mathematics is grounded in logic and entirely independent of our knowledge. Thus one cannot understand Kant's transcendental thinking if one assumes Frege's use of the concepts in question.
2. The metaphysical problem concerning the absolute totality of things in space and time, if it is to be solved, requires the possibility of making universally valid judgments about the

totality of all empirical experience. But the idea of the totality of empirical experience is not a possible object of experience, and therefore cannot be an object of an empirical judgment. The limitation described here is not however a description of the limits of human knowledge so much as a conceptual remark regarding experience and totality. The idea of the totality of things in space and time does not lend itself to the methods of sciences (which rely on distinct empirical experience), and the judgments made on the basis of the accuracy and legitimacy of those methods.

3. This article is not intended to contribute to Kant exegesis in any way, but to use certain basic elements of Kantian philosophy as a perspicuous presentation of the problems addressed herein. The question of just what Kant means by his reference to 'thoughts' and related issues are therefore not within the parameters of the present discussion. For a helpful analysis related to the issues touched upon (see Pippin, 1987).

References

Clarke, W. (2007). *Academic Charisma and the Origins of the Research University*. Chicago, IL: University of Chicago Press.
Collingwood, R. G. (2002). *An autobiography*. Oxford: Clarendon Press.
Foucault, M. (1979). *Discipline and punish: The birth of the prison*. (A. Sheridan, Trans.). New York, NY: Vintage Books.
Foucault, M. (1986). Kant on enlightenment and revolution. *Economy and Society, 15*(1), 88–96.
Hadot, P. (2002). *Philosophy as a way of life*. Oxford: Blackwell.
Kant, I. (1965). *Critique of pure reason* (N. K. Smith, Trans.). New York, NY: St. Martin's Press.
Pippin, R. (1987). Kant on the spontaneity of mind. *Canadian Journal of Philosophy, 17*, 449–475.
Pippin, R. (2006). Philosophy is its own time comprehended in thought. *Topoi, 25*, 85–90.

Doubt, Despair and Hope in Western Thought: Unamuno and the promise of education

PETER ROBERTS
College of Education, University of Canterbury

Abstract

This article examines the importance of doubt in Western philosophy, with particular attention to the work of Søren Kierkegaard and Miguel de Unamuno. Kierkegaard's pseudonymous author Johannes Climacus ventures down the pathway of doubt, finds it perplexing and difficult and discovers that he is unable to return to his pre-doubting self. In despair, the meaningfulness of his life is called into question. Unamuno, a great admirer of Kierkegaard, acknowledges the suffering that accompanies doubt while affirming the pivotal role of uncertainty, despair and struggle in realising our humanity. From Unamuno, we can acquire a keener sense of the part education has to play in both forming us as doubting beings and allowing us to work constructively with the despair engendered by this formation.

Philosophy begins with doubt: this is the central proposition explored in Søren Kierkegaard's posthumously published *Philosophical Fragments* (Kierkegaard, 1985). Through his pseudonym Johannes Climacus, Kierkegaard set out to consider the potentially destructive power of doubting in (modern) philosophy. His plan, as enunciated in the supplementary materials included with the book, was that Climacus would doubt everything, suffer greatly in doing so and, to his horror, find he is unable to return to his pre-doubting self. Life would lose its meaning for him, and he would fall into despair (pp. 234–235). The narrative that unfolds is more complex than this description suggests, but Kierkegaard remains true to his underlying idea: the principle of doubt, as interpreted, investigated and enacted by Climacus, appears to be debilitating rather than enabling. Climacus's experience is illustrative of the connection between doubt as an epistemological matter on the one hand and doubt as an ontological and ethical matter on the other. This connection has important educational implications.

Doubt and despair have continued to feature as thematically linked concerns in Western thought following Kierkegaard, particularly among writers of a broadly existentialist frame of mind. There is little agreement among existentialists themselves as to what that term means, and many who have been located within this tradition by others have expressed discomfort if not outright hostility at having the label applied to them. It is nonetheless possible to identify some key concerns in this body of work. At the heart of existentialist enquiry, whether of a literary, philosophical or theological kind, is a cluster of problems relating to the meaning of our existence as human beings. Why are we here? How do we give our lives a sense of purpose and significance? What does it mean to exist as a human being? Does God exist? Is there life after death? If there is no God, is everything permitted? What ethical principles, if any, should guide our lives? What are our obligations to others? How do we come to understand ourselves and the world? (cf. Baggini, 2004; Barrett, 1990; Cooper, 1999; Flynn, 2006; Kaufmann, 1975; Marino, 2004; Webster, 2009.)

Among the thinkers who might be considered existentialists, one who addressed these questions with a special sense of urgency was the Spanish philosopher and novelist, Miguel de Unamuno. For Unamuno (1972), doubt and despair were central elements of what he referred to as the 'tragic sense of life'. Our lives are tragic because we are beings endowed with both a longing for an immortality and the capacity to question such desires. Unamuno made it clear, however, that doubt need not be destructive; indeed, it is through uncertainty that hope arises and is given substance and significance. Seeing this more 'positive' side to doubt in Unamuno's writings is, however, no easy matter; Unamuno makes us *work* to find this, and in this sense, his task is pedagogical in nature. To understand Unamuno's position, it is helpful to have some idea of where he sits in the broader Western history of doubt as a philosophical orientation. This will be the focus of the first part of the article. The second part sketches some of Unamuno's key ideas and explores their educational ramifications. Prompted by Unamuno, I argue that doubt, contrary to Johannes Climacus's experience, can be seen in a constructive light as a pivotal element in any meaningful, worthwhile educational life.

Doubt in Western Philosophy

Doubt has served as a fundamental principle underlying philosophical investigation in the West from the time of the ancient Greeks, as exhibited by the intellectual strategies of probing, questioning, challenging and debating. Socratic conversation, to which we still pay homage in our educational, parliamentary and legal institutions, rests on the assumption that if knowledge is to advance, we must be prepared to subject our perceptions, opinions and ideas to rigorous scrutiny. This is the form of philosophical exploration undertaken by Plato in dialogues such as *The Republic* (Plato, 1974). In seeking knowledge, we must come to appreciate what we do *not* know, and the trigger in starting that process is invariably the planting of a seed of doubt. In Plato's dialogues, it was typically Socrates who assumed the role of questioner, probing persistently until views that had hitherto been taken for granted by his interlocutors were (ostensibly) left in tatters. At the same time, Plato also attempted to illustrate, most famously in the *Meno* (Plato, 1949), that if the right questions are asked, we may discover—recollect, as Plato would see it—knowledge we did not know we had.

Modern Western philosophy is often said to have started with Descartes, and Descartes begins with doubt. In his *Discourse on Method*, Descartes declares that he will 'reject as absolutely false' everything he could imagine might have any ground for doubt, to see whether anything would remain that was 'entirely certain' (Descartes, 1911, p. 101). This is the basis for his methodological scepticism, a form a philosophical enquiry still influential today. Descartes acknowledges that we can be deceived by our senses and fall prey to paralogisms in our reasoning. He resolves to treat everything that enters his mind as no more true than the illusions we construct in our dreams. 'But immediately afterwards', he says,

> I noticed that whilst I thus wished to think all things false, it was absolutely essential that the 'I' who thought this should be somewhat, and remarking that this truth 'I think, therefore I am' was so certain and so assured that all the most extravagant suppositions brought forward by sceptics were incapable of shaking it, I came to the conclusion that I could receive it without scruple as the first principle of the Philosophy for which I was seeking. (p. 101)

Across the centuries, Descartes' one apparent certainty has, of course, become rather less certain and there is now a substantial and complex body of scholarly work that calls his philosophical starting point into question. Some raise doubts about the 'I' element in the famous 'I think, therefore I am' dictum (suggesting, for example, that it might more properly be conceived as 'we'); others focus on the thinking part and argue that in seeking to understand ourselves and the world, we might just as well say 'I *feel*, therefore I am' (see Roberts, 2000). Doubt prompted Descartes, but if he hoped to find a safe haven in one proposition that could be free from such doubting, the history of Western philosophy would suggest he was mistaken. Descartes has not freed philosophers from doubt; instead, he has played his part in creating further doubt.

On the face of it, it is perfectly possible to live with few or no doubts. We can point to those who appear so certain in their political, religious or lifestyle convictions that they either cannot or will not consider alternative views. Apparent certainty in belief may arise from faith, or from 'brainwashing', or from an inability to reflect on what one holds to be true. Proclamations of the kind 'There can be little doubt ...' carry with them a tacit sense of epistemological superiority, as if it can be taken for granted that 'knowing' is always and necessarily better than 'not knowing' or 'not being certain that one knows'. There is often a quality of excessive certainty evident in such examples that many philosophers and educationists find troubling. Freire (1994, 1997) regarded such cases of being too certain of one's certainties as dogmatism and noted that this could be present among those on both the left and the right of the political spectrum. Ironically, a tendency towards excessive certainty of one kind—intellectual smugness—is not altogether unusual among those who profess to be sceptics. Scepticism, supposedly founded on doubt, can be brandished rather unreflectively as a kind of weapon, often involving a belittling of others: a sniggering attitude that betrays an underlying arrogance about the rightness of one's own position.

But what might we mean when we use terms such as 'doubt' and 'certainty'? It is not always clear where one ends and the other begins. Doubt suggests some kind of questioning and certainty implies some form of acceptance that is beyond questioning. But these thoughts invite questions of their own: What is being questioned (or not questioned)? By whom? Towards what end? If we take seriously the insights afforded by a variety of critical traditions of educational scholarship—Marxist, psychoanalytic, post-structuralist and postmodern, among others—it should be evident that the answers to such questions are seldom as straightforward as we would like to believe. If, as an expression of doubt, 'I' question, it is a matter for debate as to what constitutes the 'I'. From a number of different critical perspectives, it can be argued that we are not the authors of our own intentions. We might probe further and ask whether doubt is best understood as an *experience* of questioning or as an *expression* of questioning. Indeed, expressing doubt through questioning can often lead to greater certainty of a kind: a sharper sense of clarity about what we believe we know and do not know.

Even if there are elements of certainty in a questioning frame of mind, such a mind can never fully settle. And this is perhaps the key feature of doubt: it implies some form of *movement*. Doubt tends to breed further doubt. From a methodological perspective, systematic doubt can become, as Langer (1929) puts it, a 'treadmill':

> Everything must be doubted that possibly can be; and the really honest scholar, realising that every philosopher before him has been discredited by many competent persons, becomes wary, in the end, about believing anything, for he is no longer satisfied with the 'self-evidence' of his assumptions. He refutes his own ideas, and finally is faced with a choice between blind dogmatic beliefs, or no beliefs at all—between scepticism, or animal faith. (p. 380)

This characterisation of the 'treadmill' effect of constant doubting resonates with Climacus's experience, but Kierkegaard wants to remind us that there is more at stake here than methodological frustration. Doubting, as an intellectual orientation, has moral consequences.

In subjecting everything to doubt, we change ourselves as human beings; we create a mode of being from which there is no escape. Once formed as a doubting subject, one cannot simply dispense with fresh doubts as they arise. Once developed, a doubting consciousness prods us whether we want it to or not; it will not leave us alone, and even if we manage to push it into the background temporarily, it often rears its head again precisely when we wish it would disappear. Doubt can inhibit the formation of virtues such as trust and acceptance and in so doing undermine our relationships with others. Doubt, when taken to extremes, can be utterly debilitating, harming not only the life of the doubter but also those with whom the doubter associates. These possibilities were both theorised and exemplified, in a highly personalised way, by Miguel de Unamuno. In Unamuno's life and work, the connection between doubt and despair comes into particularly sharp focus. Doubt haunted Unamuno and exerted an influence on almost everything he wrote. But in Unamuno's failure to 'escape' from his doubts, there are also some important lessons for educationists and these will be considered in the next section.

Doubt, Despair and Hope: Unamuno and the Promise of Education

Unamuno held Kierkegaard in the highest esteem. Already multilingual, Unamuno taught himself Danish just so that he could read the man he considered an intellectual 'brother' in his original language. Kierkegaard's (1985) dissatisfaction with the modern Western philosophical account of doubt is mirrored in Unamuno's writings but expressed in more direct terms. Unamuno distinguishes between methodical doubt, as portrayed by Descartes, and passionate doubt—the 'eternal conflict between reason and feeling, between science and life, between the logical and the biotic' (Unamuno, 1972, p. 120). The former is a kind of theoretical game; the latter is crucial in defining us as human beings. For Unamuno, the quest to know, through philosophical enquiry among other means, is not merely an intellectual exercise; it is an important part of the process of giving our lives meaning, substance and purpose. Unamuno himself lived this way, desperately seeking to dispense with his doubts, but never quite succeeding in doing so. Unamuno's doubts were expressed not just to amuse himself but as a manifestation of his searching for an answer to what he saw as the most pressing question of all: the possibility of immortality. In considering Unamuno's views on doubt, then, it is also important to examine his pronouncements on matters of faith and belief.

In his classic work, *The Tragic Sense of Life*, Unamuno recognises in himself his *will* to believe in life after death, while simultaneously acknowledging the absurdity of such a belief from a purely rational point of view. He does not himself possess a simple faith that all will be well—indeed, he is driven more by nagging doubts—but he cautions against the development of a form of bitterness towards those who do see the world in these terms. He is highly critical of those rationalists who, in finding themselves unable to believe, lash out in anger at those who do have faith. This hatred, he observes, has led to the persecution of Christians, among others, and is fundamentally hypocritical. A professed commitment to rationalism can become profoundly irrational. There is also hypocrisy in the refusal among rationalists to admit that reason dissolves and disheartens (pp. 106–107). Unamuno's disdain for rationalists who exhibit these characteristics is matched by his admiration for those who strive to believe in immortality but find, in all sincerity, that they cannot. This is, he says, 'the most noble, most profound, most human and most fruitful attitude and state of mind' (p. 107). Such an attitude captures what Unamuno understands by despair. Despair is seen not as a condition to be avoided; instead, in exercising our reflective capacities as human beings, we find we *cannot* avoid it and must face up to it.

Unamuno is wary of the attempt under Catholicism, and scholastic theology in particular, to make faith conform to the dictates of reason. This has arisen, he argues, from a sense of insecurity among those who profess to believe. Faith, no longer sure of itself, 'sought to establish a foundation, not *against* reason, which is where it stands, but *upon* reason, that is, within reason itself' (p. 84). Such an enterprise,

Unamuno maintains, is doomed to failure. Reason, the 'enemy' of faith, turns back against those who seek to harness it (p. 83). Unamuno concedes that there is a price to be paid by those who believe—they must suppress what their intellect demands of them—but this is exaggerated by the 'all or nothing' approach to accepting religious dogma. To expect people to believe too much—to accept apparently absurd doctrines—not only invites scepticism but can lead to the opposite of what was intended: to the total rejection of belief. From Unamuno's perspective, the danger lies not just in believing too much but in 'attempting to believe with one's reason rather than one's life' (p. 86). Attempting to ground dogmatic theology in reason ends up not only alienating disbelievers but also failing to satisfy reason. Unamuno maintains that faith and reason will always be in tension with each other; trying to force one upon the other is, as he sees it, a fruitless exercise.

According to Unamuno, all attempts to rationalise or scientise religious belief can be traced back to the key human attribute of intelligence: 'a dreadful matter'. Intelligence 'tends towards death in the way that memory tends towards stability'. Unamuno elaborates:

> That which lives, that which is absolutely unstable, absolutely individual, is, strictly speaking, unintelligible. Logic tends to reduce everything to identities and genera, to a state where each representation has no more than one single selfsame content in whatever place, time, or relation the representation may occur to us. But nothing is the same for two successive moments of its being. My idea of God is different each time I conceive it. Identity, which is death, is precisely what the intellect seeks. The mind seeks what is dead, for the living escapes it. It seeks to congeal the flowing stream into blocks of ice. It seeks to arrest the flow. (p. 100)

He continues with these memorable words:

> In order to understand anything it must first be killed, laid out rigid in the mind. Science is a cemetery of dead ideas, even though live ideas are born out of it. Worms, also, feed on corpses. My own thoughts, tumultuous and agitated in the recesses of my mind, once torn up by their roots from my heart, poured out upon this paper and here fixed in unalterable form, are already the cadavers of thought. (pp. 100–101)

For Unamuno, neither science specifically nor reason more generally can provide the sustenance we need in responding to our underlying longing for immortality. To the contrary, reason, bounded by its own limits, leads us to the conclusion that we cannot persist. Reason is in essence sceptical. Reason, in probing and enquiring, in seeking explanations, disrupts the flow of life. Unamuno argues that, as a destructive and dissolving force, it in effect turns back on itself, casting doubt on its own validity. Like Nietzsche before him, but in a very different way, Unamuno foreshadows a key theme in twentieth century philosophical debate: the question of relativism: 'A stomach ulcer ends by causing the stomach to digest itself, and reason ends by destroying the immediate and absolute validity of the concept of truth and of the concept of necessity. Both concepts are relative: there is no absolute truth, no absolute necessity' (p. 116).

Absolute relativism, Unamuno suggests, is the 'supreme triumph of ratiocinating reason' (p. 117). In this sense, reason destroys itself and if it was possible for us to remain purely and exclusively in the embrace of reason, it would destroy us.

These claims have important educational implications. Few would deny that education is, or ought to be, concerned at least in part—and perhaps in *large* part—with the development of reason. This position has been well defended in educational philosophy, via the work of Peters, Hirst and Dearden (the 'London School'), Israel Scheffler, Harvey Siegel and many others. Unamuno's point, however, is that as living, feeling, willing human beings, we dwell not merely within the realm of reason but also outside it—in the domains of the irrational and contra-rational, the absurd and the uncertain (pp. 115–116). As Unamuno was fond of saying, 'everything vital is, not only irrational, but anti-rational, and everything rational is anti-vital' (p. 39). In his writings, Unamuno is not *against* reason; his point is rather that we must be aware of its *limits*. If we expect reason to 'resolve' the deepest problems we face as human beings, we will, Unamuno suggests, ultimately be disappointed. We must, he says, begin with ourselves—with how we exist in the world—and examine reason in relation to our longings, frustrations, hopes and interactions with others. As Unamuno puts it in commenting on Descartes:

> The defect in Descartes's *Discourse on Method* does not lie in the methodical prior doubt, in the fact that he begins by resolving to doubt everything, which is no more than a mere artifice; the defect lies in his resolving to begin by leaving himself out, omitting Descartes, the real man, the man of flesh and blood, the man who does not want to die, so that he can become a mere thinker, that is, an abstraction. But the real man reappears and works his way into the philosophy. (p. 39)

Unamuno sees great significance in Descartes's confession that prior to subjecting his beliefs and interests to the rigorous scrutiny of science and reason, he loved poetry, delighted in mathematics, thought highly of eloquence and sought to go to Heaven. In these elements of his work, Unamuno sees the real Descartes, at odds with the method he seeks to apply to himself. For Unamuno, Descartes's *cogito ergo sum* rests on a mistake: a confusion between knowing and being (in its fuller sense):

> 'I think, therefore I am' can only mean, 'I think, therefore I am a thinker'; the *being* in the *I am*, derived from *I think*, is no more than a knowing; that *being* is knowledge, not life. The primary reality is not that I think, but that I live, for those who do not think also live, even though that kind of living is not a true life. So many contradictions, dear Lord, when we try to wed life to reason! ... The truth is *sum, ergo cogito*—I am, therefore I think, though not everything that is, thinks.

As Unamuno sees it, Descartes could equally have said 'I feel, therefore I am', or 'I will, therefore I am'. When trying to understand what it means to be a human being, then, we must see thinking, feeling and willing as intertwined. We do not merely think thoughts but also feel them. And to direct our thoughts, and bring them back on task when we stray, the will must find regular exercise. For Unamuno, each of these inner elements of the human being is ultimately directed towards self-preservation of one kind or another: a continuation of our being in some form.

Unamuno's notion of continuation is directly connected to his own personal longing for immortality. He wants to survive, not in the abstract, not symbolically, not as an impersonal element absorbed into a greater divine wholeness; it is he, the man, Miguel de Unamuno, with all his shortcomings, his suffering, his fragilities, who wants to go on. In some respects, this is the great weakness of Unamuno's work: his musings on immortality, on reason, faith and feeling can seem too idiosyncratically individualistic, too self-centred. Why, it might be asked, should we take him seriously as a thinker, a philosopher, when he is, by his own admission, concerned more with *himself* than with theoretical rigour? One answer is to say that this weakness is simultaneously a strength, for it is in showing us how deeply embedded our philosophical concerns are with the most fundamental questions of human existence, as lived, that his work gains its force and significance. Unamuno will *not let us go*. He shakes us from our slumbers, his obsession with immortality reminding us of just how important the question of death, and its relationship to consciousness, is to our sense of the meaning of life. In so doing, he *teaches* us, through his own example, through the ideas he conveys in books such as *The Tragic Sense of Life*, and via the dilemmas faced, decisions made and actions taken by his characters in his novels and short stories (Unamuno, 1972, 1996, 2000). Life, Unamuno teaches us, is a constant process of *struggle*.

Unamuno returns us to the Greek roots of the term 'agony'. As Barrett (1972) points out, in contemporary English, this word is now used principally to refer to physical or emotional pain. But the Greek word *agonia* means a contest or struggle (p. 362). *Agons* were 'endurance contests staged in ancient Greece in which combatants demonstrated their skill through arduous competitive games' (Kuhlman, 1994, p. 31). Unamuno retains the idea of a battle that was implied by the Greeks, but turns this into something that speaks to the meaning of our existence as human beings. The element of pain that we still recognise in our current use of the term 'agony' becomes, for Unamuno, a constant in the process of life itself: to live is to be in agony. There is an important connection here with a point made in the first section of this article: to doubt is part of what it means to live as a human being, and doubt, like life itself, implies movement. Unamuno teaches us that we can never quite sit still; we must learn to live with an inner existential restlessness. For Unamuno, the process of searching never ends.

At first glance, these ideas may appear to hold little educational promise, but that is perhaps partly because in the West we have become so steeped in the language of reducing struggle and suffering. The aim in many contemporary educational circles often seems to be to make learning less difficult, less painful. Learning quickly and easily is typically regarded as highly desirable. Learning, we are told, should be entertaining—it should be fun. Learning is expected to enhance happiness, not diminish it (see further, Roberts, 2013a). From Unamuno, however, we can come to appreciate that if education is, in one way or another, always a matter of learning how to live, this implies that we will also learn how to struggle. And through struggle, as Aeschylus (2003) recognised long before Unamuno, we learn. This does not mean all forms of struggle are equally productive or worthwhile from an educational point of view. But for Unamuno, the forms of learning that matter most—those connected with the existential questions identified at the beginning of this article—cannot occur without struggle. If the capacity for struggle no longer exists, if we no longer have to wrestle with doubt and despair, we are, in an important sense, no longer human (Barrett, 1972, p. 362; cf. Dienstag, 2006). Unamuno helps us in fulfilling this vocation, describing his task in uncompromising terms:

> [T]he truth is that my work—my mission, I was about to say—is to shatter the faith of men, left, right and centre, their faith in affirmation, their faith in negation, their faith in abstention, and I do so from faith in faith itself. My purpose is to war on all those who submit, whether to Catholicism, or to rationalism, or to agnosticism. My aim is to make all men live a life of restless longing. (Unamuno, 1972, p. 349)

The language here is unusually insistent, almost aggressive in tone. But this is something we must face, as kindred spirits to Kierkegaard's Climacus, in going down a philosophical and pedagogical path. Education is a process of *unsettling* us as human beings. Doubt implies a kind of permanent restlessness, a state of disequilibrium and with this a sense of discomfort. In becoming educated, we learn to live with uncertainty and with suffering as well as joy. Indeed, Unamuno argues that faith, belief and commitment are not weaker but *stronger* through the experience of uncertainty.

Unamuno's starting point in considering the potential value of uncertainty is simple acknowledgement of its existence:

> [T]he fact that the sense of uncertainty, and the inner struggle of reason against both faith and the passionate longing for eternal life, together serve as the basis for action and a foundation for morals, this fact would, in the eyes of a pragmatist, justify the sense of uncertainty. But I must make clear that I do not seek out such a practical consequence in order to justify this uncertainty; it is simply that I encounter it in my inner experience. Nor do I wish nor would I wish to seek any justification for this state of inner struggle and uncertainty and longing: it is a fact, and that suffices. (p. 142)

'The most robust faith', Unamuno maintains, 'is based on uncertainty' (p. 205). Faith ultimately relies on trust in some*one*—whether this is a specific individual, or a group of people, or God as the personalisation of the Universe—who assures us of some*thing*. Faith provides the basis, the substance, for hope. In this sense, it is hope that is the higher principle. We *create* faith, Unamuno wants to say, because we hope for the existence of a God, and we come to believe in God because this is consistent with our hope for eternal life. The question of whether Unamuno himself truly believed in God has been much debated (Baker, 1990), but arguably, he is best described as an agnostic. He perhaps did not even know himself whether he believed; but what he could not deny was that he doubted. Doubting for Unamuno is not antithetical to faith but utterly consistent with it: 'Whoever believes he believes in God, but believes without passion, without anguish, without uncertainty, without doubt, without despair-in-consolation, believes only in the God-Idea, not in God Himself' (p. 211).

From Unamuno, we can learn that our appreciation of all that life has to offer is, or can be, *enhanced*, not undermined, by our understanding of pain and despair. To begin to grasp how and why this is so, we must break away from the notion of education providing a 'solution' to the problem of despair. Hughes (1978), in reflecting on the educational significance of Unamuno's work, poses the question: 'But how does one overcome the tragic sense of life?'. Unamuno's answer, he suggests, is that 'one *doesn't*; it can only be reaffirmed through perpetual doubt and struggle, and the goal of education is to "wake up the sleeping ones" to this essential human condition through the very language they speak' (p. 137). Hughes continues:

> [A]s Unamuno saw, the essence of education is in the question, not the answer. It is in uncertainty, not certainty; suffering, not happiness; pain, not joy. The triumphs of technology and the mass media are enough to put us all to sleep; education must lead not to security, but *insecurity*. This insecurity is not the garden variety found in psychological texts which inhibits the person's ability to cope with modernity, but rather that which continually prods him onward through dissatisfaction and doubt, through paradox and contradiction, to seek *true* immortality, not the blissful promises of traditional Christian after-life. Essentially, Unamuno was of one mind with the poet Dylan Thomas: 'Do not go gentle into that good night/Rage, rage against the dying of the light'. (p. 137)

Closing Remarks

In his 2009 book, *Educating for Meaningful Lives*, Scott Webster observes that 'schooling in the western world has all too often been subservient to market and political demands' (Webster, 2009, p. xiii). A concern with *educative* learning, keenly pursued as a philosophical question in the 1960s and 1970s, has given way to a dominant institutional and policy focus on training in competencies deemed 'relevant' to employment and economic advancement (pp. 3–4). Webster seeks to recover a form of educational thinking that takes 'why' questions seriously. The 'why' questions he has in mind are those relating to the meaning, significance and purpose of life. 'It is not enough', he points out, to claim that 'you need to do such and such in order to continue to sustain your existence' or 'in order for us all to live at peace together' because sooner or later we must confront a deeper question: 'why do we even exist?' (p. ix). This kind of enquiry, as we have seen in this article, is exactly what occupied Miguel de Unamuno. Webster argues that our endeavour as human beings to respond to the question 'what is the meaning of life' is 'a matter of life and death' (p. xii). Unamuno would have shared this view. Education, for Unamuno as for Webster, can be seen as the lifelong, social process of grappling with the meaning of our own existence.

Unamuno was not content with considering whether philosophy began with doubt. He wanted to ask who is doing the doubting, about what and *why*. Doubt, from Unamuno's point of view, is not merely a prompt for enquiry but a condition for realising our humanity. For Unamuno, certainty and doubt are intertwined; both rely on each other for their intelligibility. We can only have doubts about some things if we hold, even if only temporarily, other things to be true. Education creates uncertainty, but uncertainty also creates us. Unamuno's work allows us to speak of what might be called 'educational agnosticism': an orientation to the world, and to the process of learning through searching and struggle, that admits to doubts and to the forms of despair that go along with them (cf. Vernon, 2011). The reference to agnosticism need not imply a concern with spiritual questions, but has to do more with the 'why' questions identified by Webster. The agnosticism signalled here implies a willingness to question but also a recognition that we cannot question all things all the time. Against the excessive certainties of both dogmatic belief and dismissive scepticism, educational agnosticism demands a posture of radical openness. This form of openness is radical because it goes to the root of what it means to be human: if we are too quick to judge, or too ready to accept without question, or too insistent on finding 'solutions' to the problems that confront us, we cannot fulfil our task as beings who ask 'why?'. To be open in this way requires humility but not servitude, acceptance but not resignation.

Kierkegaard's answer to the despair engendered by doubt was to make a 'leap of faith' (Kierkegaard, 1987, 1989, 2009). Unamuno supported a certain kind of faith and theorised its connection with hope, but was never able to quite make the leap advocated by Kierkegaard. He *wanted* to believe, and most of all he wanted to live on, with all his faults and suffering. But he could not shake his uncertainties, and in the end, he came to see that they defined him and gave him hope. Unamuno came to accept, as far as he could accept anything, that he would always struggle. Hope for Unamuno resided not in the escape from doubt and despair but in the very possibility of these modes of human experience. Doubt and despair remind us that we are *alive*: restless, uncomfortable, moving. Education, as a process of ongoing searching, arises from doubt and creates new doubts. The 'promise' of education, or at least education of the kind implied by Unamuno's work, is that it will make life not simpler and easier but richer, more complex and often more difficult than it was before. Education opens us up to both greater suffering and the possibility of better recognising and responding to such suffering in others. It brings with it new burdens and ethical responsibilities but also the prospect of experiencing more fully the beauty and goodness that is within and all around us (see further, Roberts, 2013b; Solomon, 1999, 2002). Like Kierkegaard's Climacus, we find, in being educated, that there is no going back; we must learn to live with the new modes of understanding we develop on an educational journey. But the lenses through which we view ourselves and the world are not fixed; they continue to change and evolve as new educational experiences are integrated with those from our past. Western philosophy may begin with doubt, but Unamuno allows us to appreciate why, in committing to the process of education, we should not want that doubt to end.

THE DILEMMA OF WESTERN PHILOSOPHY

References

Aeschylus. (2003). *The Oresteia* (A. Shapiro & P. Burian, Trans.). Oxford: Oxford University Press.

Baggini, J. (2004). *What's it all about? Philosophy and the meaning of life*. Oxford: Oxford University Press.

Baker, A. F. (1990). Unamuno and the religion of uncertainty. *Hispanic Review, 58*, 37–56.

Barrett, W. (1972). Afterword: Unamuno and the contest with death. In M. de Unamuno, *The tragic sense of life in men and nations* (pp. 361–374). Princeton, NJ: Princeton University Press.

Barrett, W. (1990). *Irrational man: A study in existential philosophy*. New York, NY: Anchor Books.

Cooper, D. E. (1999). *Existentialism: A reconstruction* (2nd ed.). Oxford: Blackwell.

Descartes, R. (1911). Discourse on method. In *The philosophical works of Descartes* (E. S. Haldane & G. R. T. Ross, Trans., Vol. 1, pp. 79–130). Cambridge: Cambridge University Press.

Dienstag, J. F. (2006). *Pessimism: Philosophy, ethic, spirit*. Princeton, NJ: Princeton University Press.

Flynn, T. (2006). *Existentialism: A very short introduction*. Oxford: Oxford University Press.

Freire, P. (1994). *Pedagogy of hope*. New York, NY: Continuum.

Freire, P. (1997). *Pedagogy of the heart*. New York, NY: Continuum.

Hughes, R. (1978). Education and the tragic sense of life: The thought of Miguel de Unamuno. *Educational Theory, 28*, 131–138.

Kaufmann, W. (Ed.). (1975). *Existentialism from Dostoevsky to Sartre*. New York, NY: Plume.

Kierkegaard, S. (1985). *Philosophical fragments* (H. V. Hong & E. H. Hong, Trans.). Princeton, NJ: Princeton University Press.

Kierkegaard, S. (1987). *Either/or* (2 vols, H. V. Hong & E. H. Hong, Trans.). Princeton, NJ: Princeton University Press.

Kierkegaard, S. (1989). *The sickness unto death* (A. Hannay, Trans.). London: Penguin.

Kierkegaard, S. (2009). *Concluding unscientific postscript* (A. Hannay, Trans.). Cambridge: Cambridge University Press.

Kuhlman, E. L. (1994). *Agony in education: The importance of struggle in the process of learning*. Westport, CT: Bergin & Garvey.

Langer, S. K. (1929). The treadmill of systematic doubt. *The Journal of Philosophy, 26*, 379–384.

Marino, G. (Ed.). (2004). *Basic writings of existentialism*. New York, NY: The Modern Library.

Plato. (1949). The Meno. In Plato, *Five Dialogues* (F. Sydenham, Trans., pp. 82–132). London: Everyman's Library.

Plato. (1974). *The republic* (2nd ed., H. D. P. Lee, Trans.). Harmondsworth: Penguin.
Roberts, P. (2000). *Education, literacy and humanization: Exploring the work of Paulo Freire*. Westport, CT: Bergin and Garvey.
Roberts, P. (2013a). Happiness, despair and education. *Studies in Philosophy and Education, 32*, 463–475.
Roberts, P. (2013b). Education, faith, and despair: Wrestling with Kierkegaard. In C. Mayo (Ed.), *Philosophy of education yearbook 2013* (pp. 277–285). Urbana, IL: Philosophy of Education Society.
Solomon, R. C. (1999). *The joy of philosophy*. Oxford: Oxford University Press.
Solomon, R. C. (2002). *Spirituality for the skeptic: The thoughtful love of life*. Oxford: Oxford University Press.
Unamuno, M. de. (1972). *The tragic sense of life in men and nations* (A. Kerrigan, Trans.). Princeton, NJ: Princeton University Press.
Unamuno, M. de. (1996). *Abel Sanchez and other stories* (A. Kerrigan, Trans.). Washington, DC: Regnery Publishing.
Unamuno, M. de. (2000). *Mist: A tragicomic novel* (W. Fite, Trans.). Chicago: University of Illinois Press.
Vernon, M. (2011). *How to be an agnostic*. London: Palgrave Macmillan.
Webster, S. (2009). *Educating for meaningful lives through existential spirituality*. Rotterdam: Sense Publishers.

The Offerings of Fringe Figures and Migrants

A.-CHR. ENGELS-SCHWARZPAUL
School of Art and Design, Auckland University of Technology

Abstract

'The Western tradition', as passe-partout, includes fringe figures, émigrés and migrants. Rather than looking to resources at the core of the Western tradition to overcome its own blindnesses, I am more interested in its gaps and peripheries, where other thoughts and renegade knowledges take hold. It is in the contact zones with strangers that glimpses of any culture's philosophical blindness become possible and changes towards a different understanding of knowledge can begin. In the context of education, I am above all interested in PhD candidates who wish to draw on the bodies and modes of knowledge they bring with them to the university. Some are not well represented: Indigenous and other non-Western traditions, non-English languages, and the renegade knowledges of marginalised groups. My context is that of creative practice-led PhD theses at AUT University, Auckland (Aotearoa/New Zealand) which have made me aware of the importance of cosmopolitics *to understand education in the context of entangled histories of colonisation and domination; border-crossing interdependencies; new types of conflict and new ways of building communities. My study thus explores aspects of transculturation—involving not only ethnic cultures (often the default understanding of culture) but also different disciplinary knowledge cultures. The place that no-one owns in Western tradition, the place of fringe figures, émigrés and migrants, may offer a point from which non-traditional candidates' thoughts can lever off to build connections with their own stores of knowledge. (Non-traditional candidates belong to minorities in Western universities until about thirty years ago when traditional candidates were 'male, from high-status social-economic backgrounds, members of majority ethnic and/or racial groups, and without disability'.) This usually means for Western supervisors that they need to recognise their ignorance towards parts of their own traditions, as well as those of their candidates. The proposition I will explore is that the emergent research of non-traditional candidates can thrive on gaps and on the fringes—provided that both candidates and supervisors are able to be porous to the unknown and 'troubled by the presumption of equality'. The potential of the gap, the unknown, which simultaneously separates and connects candidates and supervisors, can be the beginning of generating a thing in common. This is a rich and creative place for new thought, which may open the academy to transcultural knowledge.*

THE DILEMMA OF WESTERN PHILOSOPHY

To speak of the *offerings* of fringe figures and migrants implies an engagement, if only by contrast. *Offering's* antonyms are *refusal* or *withdrawal*. *Offering* also implies movement (L. *ob* 'to' + *ferre* 'to bring, to carry'), an engagement with something left behind or not yet accessed, the transfer of something to be presented in a new context (L. *offerre* 'to present, bestow, bring before'). This mobile, engaged presentation, I propose, raises issues concerning more than one intellectual tradition, cultural configuration, or language. Fringe figures, émigrés and migrants always contribute (L. *con-* 'with' + *tribuere* 'bestow') to a society or culture—even after they have left. I base this proposition on the literature as well as on my own experiences and observations. Both suggest that insights into situations, strategies and chances of success grow along with the knowledge of more than one society, culture, language and tradition. The crises often associated with the transitions from one to the other can strengthen determination, confidence and independent action, and a lack of familiarity with the dominant culture can amplify the recognition of contradictions.

The Western Tradition

Since I was born and raised in Germany, 'the Western tradition' is my own starting point. I was for the first time confronted with a non-European tradition and a non-European language when I migrated to Aotearoa/New Zealand in the early 1980s, in my twenties. The immediate experience of Māori culture, in all its differences and similarities, caused shock, and Te Reo Māori (Māori language), as a very different 'window on the world', opened new vistas. This was the first step in a gradual estrangement from my own culture and history, an estrangement Gilroy regards as essential for a critical knowledge of one's own society (2005, p. 67). My PhD, undertaken much later at the University of Auckland, was another. Originally conceived in Germany, the thesis developed decidedly local inflexions during explorations of European/Pacific connections. As it neared completion, I realised in hindsight that a large proportion of the writers I had chosen to engage with were fringe figures, many of them Jewish refugees who left Germany during the Nazi regime: Theodor W. Adorno, Hannah Arendt, Walter Benjamin, Ernst Bloch, Ernst Cassirer, Norbert Elias, Sigmund Freud and Ernst Gombrich. All were, at various stages of their lives, dissidents and migrants.

A conjunction of experience and theorising is apparent in Arendt's themes of *plurality* and *natality*. Likewise, Benjamin's concepts and theories were influenced by his experiences as émigré and migrant. Their examples show how 'the Western tradition', as passe-partout, includes liminal figures. Today, the gaps and peripheries of traditions, where other thoughts and renegade knowledges take hold, are equally or even more significant. Authors such as Gilroy (2005) and Honig (2006) explore the potentials of agonistic forms of cosmopolitanism that thrive on exposure to otherness and place great store on virtues like listening and friendship; Baecker (2012) and Beck and Grande (2010) highlight the contributions of pluralistic reflexivity to European society; Gunew (2013) and Todd (2010) link these forms of cosmopolitics to education. Finally, Jacques Rancière's writings concerning that Ignorant Schoolmaster, Jean-Joseph Jacotot (1770–1840), who fled to Belgium during the Bourbon Restoration in France (1991, 2010), are of interest.[1]

The choice of authors with experiences and theories of liminal existence in my PhD was not a conscious strategy but based on intuitive elective affinities. These writers knew 'the Western tradition' I set out from, and to which they contributed after the end of the Nazi regime, as well as the many transitions between departure and arrival in a new society. Their writing was relevant for my exploration and theorising of 'New Zealand culture'. Soon after my arrival, I had become aware that there was no such thing as a New Zealand culture. The concept was either too exclusive (e.g. for white settlers only) or meaningless (e.g. not recognising the autonomy of Māori culture). As an outsider, I noticed increasingly how mainstream New Zealand culture was blind to its own condition: white settler society lacked the identity it so desperately sought, precisely because it considered its culture as normal. Yet, a little more than 140 years earlier, the designation 'Māori' resulted from the new relationships between Tangata Whenua (Indigenous 'people of the land') and the immigrants (Pākehā or Tangata Tiriti, people of the Treaty): 'māori' means normal, ordinary or common. By the 1980s, Māori had become the Other of (white) New Zealanders.

By contrast, Māori attitudes towards immigrants during early contact were characterised by interest: many rangatira (chiefs) were keen to have their resident Pākehā–Māori (Bentley, 1999) to enhance their status and wealth and also to mediate the settlers' knowledge and culture. Māori engaged with the strangers' religion, language, literature, technology, science and economics—and a number of Pākehā immersed themselves in Māori culture. Over subsequent decades, though, the relationship between Tangata Whenua and Tangata Tiriti changed. From the perspective of contemporary settler society, Māori had become fringe figures and strangers. Their visibility in their own country decreased, as it were, along with their version of a common world. Before the so-called Māori renaissance, they became visible in the media usually through sports and cultural performances or criminal offending. In the 1980s, they became increasingly visible due to the uncomfortable challenges they began to mount to the prevailing configuration of the sensible, that is, the settler society's claim to normality.[2] Māori dissent made visible that what counted as self-evident facts resulted from the contingent distribution of parts and positions, starting with in-or exclusion in the national community.

As I developed my English language capacity and began to learn Māori in the 1980s, new worlds spread out before me, in which teachers, houses, aunts, friends, ancestors, mountains, rivers, ships, dogs and fridges behaved and related in ways I had not known before.

Visibilities

A culture's philosophical blindness can be glimpsed more easily in the contact zones with strangers, where changes towards a different understanding of knowledge can begin (Baecker, 2012; Beck & Grande, 2010; Gilroy, 2005; Gunew, 2013). Locals learn to imagine themselves as strangers through sustained contact with different perspectives on their social and cultural normality. They achieve a creative degree of estrangement from the culture into which they were born and which seems so normal (and thereby invisible or, at least, difficult to describe). It becomes obvious that the constant expectations to comply, directed by mainstream society at liminal figures, serve neither party. Obedience yields assimilation, which reduces the spaces of possibility arising from the consciousness of a gap between established order and fringe. Such consciousness supports vital and mutually productive explorations. Hannah Arendt's consciousness of otherness, for example (she lived much of her life in limbo and knew from experience what it means to be fringe figure, émigré, migrant and immigrant), afforded her with 'an exceptionally clear view of civilization' (Goultschin, 2014, p. 279). Shared with others in friendliness, such view helps develop the 'carefully cultivated degree of estrangement' by which to recognise blind spots in one's culture, that is, to see where people cannot see that they do not see what they cannot see (Baecker, 2012, p. 109). As a case in point, Beck and Grande observe that certain European fallacies can only be uncovered by looking through non-European eyes (Beck & Grande, 2010, p. 424).

In Jacques Rancière's terms, every society or group has a specific *distribution of the sensible*, which can be re-partitioned by disagreement between the established, institutionalised order and those outside or on its fringes. When that happens, aspects hitherto indiscernible can rise into visibility. For example, what is now termed a 'deficit model' (Cunningham, 2011; Ryan & Zuber-Skerritt, 1999; Slee, 2010) was regarded as a progressive, socially responsible way of considering students with cultural, physical, cognitive and other disadvantages until a controversy arose. Even today, there is much talk about the fact that, increasingly, ESOL students do not speak and write English sufficiently to succeed. While this is often correct, what is not commonly discussed is the fact that many of their teachers are mono-lingual. As a consequence, they cannot appreciate the epistemological advantages of their bi- or multi-lingual students,[3] which is 'normal' in an environment where the prevailing language, English, and the prevailing culture, Anglo-European, are presumed to establish the common world.[4]

Thus, the estrangement from one's culture fosters alternative ways of seeing. Even if the Nazis had not forced Benjamin to emigrate because he was a Jew, he would probably still have been a fringe figure, an internal émigré as it were, within Germany, rather than a normal citizen with a family and his own home. However, his exilic experiences prompted a questioning and thinking that might have never happened had he been fully integrated into German society. He wrote in a letter, 'my life no less than my thought moves in extreme positions', and the 'freedom to juxtapose things and ideas that are supposed to be incompatible, depends for its specific manifestation on danger' (in Eiland & Jennings, 2014, p. 431). Becoming émigré also entailed turning renegade for Benjamin, Arendt and many other refugees from Nazi Germany. Arendt, particularly, preserved the disagreement of the renegade as immigrant to the USA: she stood to differ, and her commitment to the 'preservation of otherness', as Moshe Gouldschin puts it, can be traced back to the connections she had formed with Benjamin in the 1930s (2014, p. 283). Significantly, Benjamin called the project of preserving otherness, 'friendliness' (*Freundlichkeit*, Benjamin, 1998, pp. 72–74). Friendliness, as the 'minimum programme of humanity' (entailing a considered and continued maintenance of distance between human beings), 'brings that distance to life' (p. 73). Arendt's notions of plurality, politics and the creation of a public sphere all rely on the maintenance of distance and the productive use of alienation and difference.

What is visible and sayable in any culture (this refers not only ethnic cultures, often the default understanding of culture, but also to different disciplinary knowledge cultures, for example) also depends on context. When different cultures confront each other in transculturation, that is, partially merge and create something new (Ortiz), the configuration of the visible changes and, with it, what can be said about it (Rancière, 2003, S5). The gap between the participants in such situations, the place in Western tradition that no-one owns, can provide non-traditional candidates' thoughts with a point from which to lever off and build connections between their own and the institution's knowledge.[5]

Pedagogies

Overwhelmingly, Western institutional education is oriented towards individual achievements, with a strong competitive slant. However, there have also been many approaches and pedagogies within Western culture that thrived in the gaps or on the fringes of state education (for example, the *Ècoles modernes* or Modern Schools of Celestine Freinet, or the twentieth century *Freie Schulen* or Free Schools of, e.g. Montessori, Pestalozzi, Steiner or Neil). All these pedagogues considered radical changes to the traditional, authoritarian and scholastic pedagogy of their times necessary, if children were to access and participate equally in a democratic world.[6]

Rancière claims that, despite manifest differences in demonstrated knowledge, the same intelligence is at work everywhere. When students arrive at the educational institution, they have already demonstrated, by learning their mother tongue, that they have the 'capacity to learn something without being taught' (Pelletier, 2012, p. 616). Rather than an end to be achieved, equality is a point of departure for Rancière. By contrast, most of our educational institutions presuppose inequality, and their deficit models target students with short fallings for remedial actions. Equality, then, has to be enacted, and it is enacted, through dissensus, which is 'not primarily a quarrel, but … a gap in the very configuration of sensible concepts, a dissociation introduced into the correspondence between ways of being and ways of doing, seeing and speaking' (Rancière, 2010, p. 15). Dissensus disrupts the routines of our perception and interpretation and constructs a stage, in Rancière's terms, or an in-between, in Arendt's.[7]

These spaces of appearance continuously change when people claim their place. As global movements between countries and across disciplines increase, and changes in political constellations and personal life styles admit more non-traditional candidates and supervisors into the academy, 'the global other is in our midst' (Beck & Grande, 2010, p. 418). Increasingly, too, domestic PhD candidates wish to draw on the bodies and modes of knowledge they bring with them to the University, which are often not

THE DILEMMA OF WESTERN PHILOSOPHY

well represented: Indigenous and other non-Western traditions, non-English languages and the renegade knowledges of marginalised groups. Consequently, situations in which a supervisor cannot directly convey knowledge relevant to a candidate's research are proliferating everywhere.

My experiences in the supervision of several non-traditional candidates in the last years have highlighted the importance of *cosmopolitics* (Honig, 2006; Todd, 2010). They open onto the dependencies and 'entanglements of histories of colonisation and domination', 'border-transcending dynamics, dependencies, interdependencies and intermingling', and 'new conflict structures, conflict dynamics and new processes of community building' (Beck & Grande, 2010, p. 411). In this situation, a move away from highly personal and private styles of supervision (which incidentally can breed dependencies and undetected interpersonal problems) may encourage more open, collaborative and democratic styles of supervision. Amongst the PhD candidates with whom I have worked in the last years are Moana Nepia (choreographer, dancer and visual artist from Ngāti Porou), Azadeh Emadi (spatial designer and video maker from Iran), Albert Refiti (Samoan born architectural theorist) and Fleur Palmer (architect from Te Rarawa/Te Aupouri). None of their projects fit into mainstream paradigms, and they are sometimes difficult to carry out. Moana, Azadeh and Fleur's PhDs are practice-led, Albert's is fully written. In each case, I had adequate expertise in parts of the project, but not in others.

Moana investigated strategies for innovation and creativity within Māori visual and performing arts. His creative practice-led PhD thesis, *Te Kore—Exploring the Māori concept of void* (2013b), crossed several disciplines, only one of which was established at AUT. As a consequence, his 2009 application for confirmation of candidature was largely misunderstood by the reviewers—a signal to Welby Ings and me, as supervisors, that a more explicit positioning was required. Accordingly, beyond the discussion of precedents, the literature in the field, the practical submission and its contribution to knowledge, Moana's exegesis contained an extensive discussion of the grounds and details of his methodology, *aratika*. Aratika (ara 'pathway, approach' + -tika 'appropriate, correct') drew upon iwi (tribe) and hapu (subtribe) knowledge traditions. One of the examiners described the methodology as 'creatively conceived and negotiated', offering 'a model for other doctoral candidates involved in creative practice'. Another examiner commented that the involvement of 'Māori principles as an artistic strategy was productive' in generating original and distinctive works that 'bore within them the marks of their origins'. Moana's greater emphasis, post confirmation of candidature, on mātauranga Māori (Māori knowledge) meant for me as supervisor that I knew even less about his research field and methods. This was scary, also in the face of a prevailing consensus amongst colleagues about the importance and necessity of a tight fit between candidates and supervisors' research fields.

This perspective, though, only considers the dyadic relationship between supervisor and candidate, not those a candidate may have with other members of the 'learning alliance' (Halse & Bansel, 2012, p. 384). Particularly at PhD level, candidates come with substantial resources of relevant and refined knowledge in their field, often gleaned from experience outside of the University. Crucially, they may belong to networks of distributed knowledge they can activate when needed. This was particularly clear in Moana's case; he is extremely well connected in several intersecting worlds of, for example, choreographers, dance practitioners, visual artists, managers, academics, peer researchers and Māori tribal repositories of knowledge. To strengthen the latter connection, we appointed an additional, Māori supervisor, Wiremu Kaa. Moana now holds a professorial position at the University of Hawai'i, following his very successful examination in December 2012.

Azadeh immigrated to Aotearoa/New Zealand in 2003, switching languages and cultural context. With Bachelor and Masters' degrees in Spatial Design completed, she enrolled in a practice-led PhD thesis in 2010. The thesis, *Motion within motion: investigating digital video in light of Substantial Motion* (2014), is informed by Persian/Islamic and Deleuzian philosophical concepts. Her video practice explores the conjunction between pixel/frame and individuals/communities in a realm of transnational moving images. With Azadeh, I started out as a truly ignorant supervisor, but we soon enjoyed the support of two secondary supervisors, Prof. Laura Marks (Simon Frazer University, Vancouver) and Dr Geraldene Peters (AUT). The geographical distribution of her supervisory team sometimes generated additional complexities. Thus, on her return from a two months visit to Vancouver, during which she almost exclusively read and discussed core texts with Laura Marks, Azadeh wanted to increase the written, scholarly part of her thesis—her practice was suspended and scholarship drove her thesis. In the process of clarifying the relationship between scholarship and practice, we attempted to create a thing in common by diagramming the territory of her thesis to reposition practical modes of investigation. As the latter regained importance, Azadeh started to think through practice again and the proportions of theory and practice in her thesis were readjusted. As I write, Azadeh has just been awarded her PhD, after an exhilarating oral defence. She was congratulated by one of the examiners for 'an exemplary creative practice PhD project' that 'combines theory and practice' symbiotically, in a way 'not easy to achieve', so that 'it is the holistic body of written and creative work that makes the thesis'. My role in Azadeh's project was obviously not that of a conveyor of knowledge; rather, it was about challenging Azadeh to stay with her project and to make informed decisions about the orientation and processes of her thesis project.

Albert is about to complete his fully written PhD, *Mavae and Tofiga: Spatial Exposition of Samoan Architecture*, which concerns Samoan concepts of space, particularly as they relate to the *faletele* (guesthouse). The *faletele*, according to Albert, not only acts as an apparatus that corrals, binds, holds and signals the rituals and identity of the extended group (*aiga*); it also creates connections with *Lagi* (the cosmos) by collecting, binding, knotting, looping, braiding, weaving, wrapping and extending architectural elements to capture the cosmos within its interior. Albert grapples with the (dis)placement of aspects of knowledge of Samoan lifeworlds within the general, Western-dominated world of knowledge. Of necessity a renegade at times, he explores the potentials this position offers to act and speak from *another* position that highlights incommensurabilities within any single determining ontological position. Co-supervisor Dr Ross Jenner and I have been constantly challenged into constructing meeting grounds with Albert, juxtaposing concepts and theories, in the process of which new ones arose. What I know today about Samoan cultures of space and fabrication,

I have learned during our collaborations. Crucially, these collaborations involved three visits to Albert's territory, Upolu.

Finally, Fleur is about half-way through her practice-led PhD thesis, *Papakāinga development: Negotiating on contested ground. Māori self-determination and assertion of tino rangatiratanga in building sustainable communities.* Her project involves participatory action research in her tribal area, Te Rawara, which is difficult to accommodate within mainstream ethics committee regulations. Fleur, too, increasingly sees herself as a renegade, or at least as someone who moved to the fringes of her accustomed field of knowledge. Consequently, Fleur decided to relocate her research from the School of Art and Design to Te Ara Poutama, the Faculty of Māori Development, where she hopes to find better institutional support in Māori environments. As a consequence, my role has changed from that of primary to secondary supervisor. Fleur's case highlights even further the importance of epistemological modesty in cross-cultural, transdisciplinary and participatory research projects: supervisors can never assume the relevance of their expertise.

This does not mean they are superfluous. Rancière has little to say about the conditions under which an ignorant supervisor supports a candidate in obtaining knowledge that is, at the outset, unknown to both. 'Jacotism is not an educational idea that one could apply to systemic school reform.' (Bingham, Biesta, & Rancière, 2010, p. 14) He only states that a distinction must be made to enable judgement and action in confusing situations: if knowledge is transmitted in the relationship between teacher and student, it must not be with set expectations of the ways in which students will take hold of the knowledge put at their disposal (Rancière & Stamp, 2011, p. 245).[8] But, in the relationship between teacher and student, the teacher's task is to oblige the student to exercise her own intelligence, a capacity she already possesses, and to send her down a path of discovery.[9]

Supervisors still have a lot to do, as critical respondent, guide and/or midwife, to help unfold the territory and path of discovery: epistemological context and appropriate structures and contexts. They can greatly assist in translating expectations and requirements of ethnic, institutional and disciplinary cultures, and they can make their knowledge and expertise available, 'to be, for an other, the source of an enacted equality' (Bingham et al., 2010, p. 14). To succeed, they need to understand that students whose mother tongue is not the 'language of instruction' at their university, for instance, have not only already demonstrated that they can learn without instruction; by learning another language they have also opened up another world, with its own ways of being and knowing, and acquired the distinct epistemological advantage of comparing and questioning both their original world and the new. Similarly, most sexual minority students have accumulated experiences of difference, alienation and stigmatisation, long before they enter the university, that cause them to question prevailing standards and information. Students from non-Western traditions, for whom family and community connections are equally or more important as individual goals, might resonate with Arendt's notions of plurality and find them helpful in coming to terms with the discrepancy between Western frameworks and their own (Lane, 1997, p. 168).

Crisis and criticality share a common root, *krínein*—divide, separate, decide—meaning both 'subjective critique' and 'objective crisis' (Isenberg, 2012). Crises force into view questions that seem to have already been answered, to the point of congealing into prejudice; crises are undetermined, call for 'decisions, distinctions and discernment' (Isenberg, 2012). They are catastrophic only when they trigger prejudice (Arendt, 1961, p. 174); otherwise, they stimulate explorations beyond the apparent, new beginnings, bold and fresh ideas. Unsurprisingly, then, candidates who have experienced profound crises have frequently developed habits of sustained questioning, seeking validation of knowledge and pronounced independence (Ings, 2013). Likewise, people whose actions move them out of their accustomed territory, who have had to relearn to live life differently, often experience paradigm shifts concerning their understanding of what is possible in the world (Lane, 1997, p. 165).

Thus, 'the one who is supposedly ignorant in fact already understands innumerable things' (Rancière, 2010, p. 5). Whether the institution can respond to this adequately depends on its self-understanding: as an establishment, it is something fixed and beyond the influence of students; as the living part of this establishment, it is a cluster of 'processes, creative phenomena, meaning-making activities or supports' that is much more amenable to change and collaboration (Pesce, 2011, p. 1146). In this form, an institution is more likely to recognise the value of non-traditional candidates and renegades' challenges to the validity and value of institutional standards and concerns in preventing insincere assimilation of difference, for the sake of monetary or political gains. The latter too often leads to a negligent benevolence characteristic of many inclusion programmes (targeted at women, Indigenous, coloured, ESOL, SEN, sexual minority students and so on). Already, practice-led theses are becoming a hot new product in the universities' competitive diversification. In New Zealand, international fees and double funding for Māori and Pacific postgraduate theses completions link these candidatures directly to institutional economic gains—without automatically improving the candidates' conditions of study. The latters' questioning can counteract these tendencies by revealing the contingent nature of any configuration of sensible concepts, including the relationship between pedagogical and social logic (see Rancière, 2010, p. 1). Candidates such as Moana and Azadeh provide, in a climate of institutional harmonisation, a 'transgressive will' when they act 'as if intellectual equality were indeed real and effectual' (Rancière, 2004, p. 219)—a necessary dissonance throwing different epistemologies into focus.[10]

Between non-European and new and emerging research approaches, new modes of knowledge are inaugurated. To some extent, candidates undertaking creative practice-led research still operate on the fringes of many traditional Western universities. Non-traditional candidates, who can make unique contributions to our common body of knowledge, negotiate academic engagements across several intersecting worlds. Frequently imbedded in diverse, even contradictory webs of experience, they may not feel fully at home anywhere, neither on the absolute margin nor at the centre of their academic tribe (see Disch, 1994, p. 23). They struggle to have their 'distinctiveness recognised as an excellence' rather than 'a deviation from existing norms'. Eventually, though, they may well 'redefine the standards by which distinctiveness is recognised' (Disch, 1994, p. 57). This is precisely what happened to Moana over the course of his PhD project (see Nepia, 2013a, p. 19). Azadeh, Albert and Fleur, similarly, self-consciously occupy marginal positions and want their distinctiveness to be validated as potential excellence.

At least for now, non-traditional candidates are likely to work with supervisors who are not quite at home with their research agendas. In those cases, supervisors can best offer support by assuming a position of epistemological modesty (Arendt, 1992, p. 33; Barone, 2008, p. 35) to make room for creative links between non-traditional candidates' interests and dispositions and the concerns of non-traditional fields of knowledge or research. Otherwise, supervisors who do not fully understand the complexity of non-traditional research contexts and positions risk pulling the contextual/theoretical focus into their own fields of expertise, away from their candidates' frameworks and interests (Ho, 2013, p. 84). The uncertainty inherent in non-traditional thesis projects requires supervisors and candidates to appreciate each other's capacities and to be open to mutual education.[11]

Resources and Friendship

Before concluding, I would like to address important issues of resources and friendliness, which are insufficiently considered in Rancière's account. The first is almost exclusively addressed through a 'thing in common' between teacher and students. For Jacotot, it was the *Télémaque*, a bi-lingual book he gave his students to work with: 'placed between two minds', it served not only as a source of information, but as a gauge of equality, a source of material verification, and a bridge—a passage and a distance maintained (Rancière, 1991, p. 32).[12] In creative practice-led research projects, it is often the most current piece of practice, in fully written theses a chapter draft, and in all cases, it can be a doodle, diagram, image, sound or text.[13] Equally emphatic about the need to maintain distance, Arendt refers to a 'world of things', of human artefacts and fabrications. They are located between actors in a common world, simultaneously relating and separating them (Arendt, 1958/1998, p. 52). The distance affords, in the best case, an opening for different positions to generate diverse and productive encounters and perspectives; the thing in common repositions all involved. According to Arendt, the appearance of worldly reality relies on 'the simultaneous presence of innumerable perspectives and aspects' (p. 57).

In my experience, outcomes produced in the context of the thesis are things in common. Apart from the candidates' theses proper, I would also include occasional collaborations between candidates and supervisors on workshops, papers or publications. During Moana's initiation of PhD research with a four-day wānanga (School of Learning) in Tokomaru Bay, for instance, I was both participant observer and cook. Partaking in discussions of choreographed pieces and video experiments at the outset of the project was immensely helpful in understanding later developments, and the shared experiences created a common ground supporting our supervisory relationship to the end. With Azadeh, various types of things in common were indispensable to the generation of new potentialities: visiting her in Tehran, and our shared travel to Isfahan, triggered a subtle but substantial shift in understanding. Jointly producing diagrams of her work, at the critical point of determining the relationship between the written and the practice part of her exegesis, was another instance.[14] Azadeh and I also coauthored an article reflecting on threshold experiences in PhD research and supervision (Engels-Schwarzpaul & Emadi, 2011), which involved us in extensive discussions about appropriate epistemologies and metaphors, particularly as her PhD research project spans four different continents. This joint production generated a common space in which our mutual understanding of the research contexts as potentiality and new beginnings grew, and in which we were repositioned in relation to each other (Masschelein, 2011, p. 532).

The relationships created by things in common, particularly if made by the participants themselves, feature in many alternative pedagogies as resources for collective exploration and learning, experimental testing, and communication with outsiders.[15] Insofar as things in common give rise to dialogue and discussion in and beyond the supervisory team, they tend to draw into the project the candidates' networks of peers and outside advisors as an important resource. Supervisors then become a resource amongst many others—a calming thought when considering the increasing possibility of their ignorance *vis à vis* their candidates' projects. Hans-Georg Gadamer remarked that a common language is first worked out in conversations around something that is placed at the centre. The participants, rather than simply adjusting their tools or adapting to each other, 'come under the influence of the truth of the object and are thus bound to one another in a new community'. Understanding in dialogue, then, 'is not merely a matter of putting oneself forward and successfully asserting one's own point of view, but being transformed into a communion in which we do not remain what we were' (1975, p. 371).[16]

To many supervisors, non-traditional candidates are strangers (e.g. national, ethnic, gender or disciplinary). The supervisory contact zone provides them with a chance to obtain a degree of estrangement from their own (national, ethnic, disciplinary, etc.) culture, which helps developing a sense for their own blind spots and a different understanding of knowledge. Beyond tolerance of difference, the presumption of equal value and complexity makes room for more active engagements with the unknown than are likely to occur in multiculturalist frameworks or through the consideration of some generalised Other. Gilroy holds that demotic forms of cosmopolitanism find 'civic and ethical value in the process of exposure to otherness' and glory 'in the ordinary virtues and ironies—listening, looking, discretion, friendship—that can be cultivated when mundane encounters with difference become rewarding' (2005, p. 70). In these 'exciting transcultural possibilities' (Manathunga, 2013), a friendliness can develop that is neither unreflected nor casual but based on mutual interest and respect. It not only preserves the distance between human beings but brings it to life, in the liminal space of possibility arising from the encounter (Benjamin, 1998, p. 73). In supervisory relationships between those established in the university and those who arrive, pass through or even plan to leave the university, this vitality of uncompromised autonomy creates an opening for different perspectives and ways of thinking, embodied in heterogeneous languages, sciences and cultural narratives.[17]

The emergent research of non-traditional candidates thrives on gaps and on the fringes—provided both candidates and supervisors are able to be porous to the unknown and 'troubled by the presumption of equality' (translator's note in Rancière, 2010, p. 24). The potential of the gap, the unknown, which simultaneously separates and connects candidates and supervisors, institutes the beginning of a thing in common. This is a rich and creative place for new thought, an opening for the academy to transcultural knowledge.

Notes

1. If I take liberties in discussing Benjamin, Arendt and Rancière in concert, without also explicating their differences, I follow Benjamin's notion of claiming the 'freedom to juxtapose things and ideas that are supposed to be incompatible' (in Eiland & Jennings, 2014, p. 431). Rancière has on several occasions stated his disagreement with both Arendt and Benjamin. However, there are parallels between Arendt and Rancière, as 'thinkers of ruptural and inaugurative politics with a particularly spatial conceptualisation of politics' as a world building activity and with spaces of appearance (e.g. their orientation by praxis, the construction of space for acting together, their focus on process and performance rather than identity, see Dikeç, 2013). In my understanding, Rancière's disagreements with Arendt concern primarily matters that lie outside the scope of discussion here (see Dikeç, 2013; Schaap, 2011). His disagreement with Benjamin, as I understand it, hinges on a different definition of *aesthetics*—their deployment of this term operates mostly at different levels. Like some writers (e.g. Balibar and Ingram), I prefer to see similarities and shared potentials, rather than differences that seem irrelevant in this context.
2. The configuration or distribution of the sensible denotes the prevailing 'overall relation between ways of being, ways of doing and ways of saying', seeing and hearing (Rancière, 2010, p. 8) that regulate visibility.
3. In *Ignorance and pedagogies of intellectual equality*, Michael Singh and Xianfang Chen (Singh & Chen, 2011) show how, in a four-part process of *challenge, conceptualise, contextualise* and *connect*, hegemonic Western concepts can be replaced by new ones that are generated through the exploration of Chinese metaphors, creating transcultural relationships advancing common understanding (Singh & Chen, 2011). Similarly, Moana Nepia worked with Māori concepts and narratives to generate an innovative methodology for his creative practice-led doctoral research.
4. That teachers often do not know as much about their own culture and history as they assume, and less than some outsiders, complicates matters. Challenges to these assumptions might render visible an unexpected lack of familiarity on the part of many educators with the gaps, twists and fissures of the dominant culture and history. It may become clear that the common world is made up by more than the dominant culture.

5. Non-traditional candidates belong to minorities in Western universities until about thirty years ago when traditional candidates were 'male, from high-status social-economic backgrounds, members of majority ethnic and/or racial groups, and without disability' (Taylor & Beasley, 2005, p. 141).
6. Arendt is surprisingly conservative when it comes to education: whereas political action is the freedom to 'change every constellation' (Arendt, 1958/1998, p. 190), education is, first and foremost, about creating a place for newcomers in the common world (Curtis, 2001, p. 134).
7. Arendt would call this in-between a 'space of appearance' in which we can act in concert with others (Arendt, 1998, pp. 199, 244).
8. Arendt has a similar concern: 'Our hope always hangs on the new which every generation brings; but precisely because we can base our hope only on this, we destroy everything if we so try to control the new that we, the old, can dictate how it will look' (Arendt, 1961, p. 192).
9. Sugata Mitra, instigator of the 'Hole-in-the-Wall' experiment, in which Tamil speaking groups children learnt to browse a computer without receiving any instructions from outside, describes this relationship as one where a 'friendly mediator … provides supervision but exercises minimal intervention (encouraging rather than teaching)' (Mitra & Dangwal, 2010, p. 685). Rancière's position is frequently misunderstood to mean that a supervisor will be the better the less she knows about the subject; it is certainly based on 'a thoroughgoing resistance to a certain form of epistemological and ontological mastery' (Chambers, 2012, p. 639). Prof. Mark Dorrian, now at the University of Edinburgh, suggested in an interview that a supervisor who is 'not necessarily an expert' might be more open to 'a different kind of approach to the subject matter' in (Jenner, 2013, p. 216).
10. When equality becomes performative in the affirmation that Western and non-Western traditions are equal in depth, scope and complexity, dissonances are often the result. While the day-to-day efforts to improve educational contexts leave little space for these dissonances, paying attention to them from time to time helps keeping the contingency of our normality in view (Rancière, 2010, p. 16). In any event, all traditions of thought have much to gain form these engagements. There is probably no single method for this process, since it must grow out of each unique constellation in which it arises.
11. I have noticed that twinges of uncertainty and anxiety can make me close down and become rigid. A supervisor interviewed by Christine Halse (2011, p. 563) reflected that fear of non-completion can incline supervisors towards spoon feeding and filling deficient areas with *Spakfilla*, particularly when faced with intensifying accountability regimes. This is unsustainable: graduates eventually realise that they have not acquired the knowledge needed. A different scholarly identity for both supervisors and candidates, involving collaboration, interdependence, and an appreciation of each other's specific capacities, would always see knowledge in the diverse contexts of its production and distribution (Halse & Bansel, 2012, p. 388).
12. Rancière contrasts explicator-instructors with artists, whom he sees more closely aligned with equality and common action. His consideration of the pedagogical relationship takes place, though, in a tightly vertical, hierarchical atmosphere. By contrast, Hannah Arendt explores horizontal difference between equals in the public realm, the common world. We constantly co-produce this in-between, which relates and separates us at the same time, gathering us *and* providing distance that 'prevents our falling over each other' (Arendt, 1958/1998, p. 52). Imagine that European books might have played a similar role to that of the *Telemaque* in Jacotot's class room during early immigration to New Zealand—a thing in common not only between immigrants and Māori but between Māori teachers and students (Head & Mikaere, 1988, p. 19).
13. King Tong Ho recommends the early production of glossaries and various forms of documentation, to create a shared vocabulary and context (2013, p. 89). Useful for consultation and mutual education, these *things in common* act as material references at various stages in

the exploration and testing of different ideas. Later, as part of the exegesis, they may provide a focusing device for examiners.
14. Arendt's notion of training 'one's imagination to go visiting' (1992, p. 43) and to think from standpoints not one's own is also useful. The space of the visiting imagination is 'open to all sides' and allows our particular conditions to stand next to those of our hosts—never becoming the same, though—and always maintaining their distance. Across those distances, our common world—'not a given but produced as a result of visiting' (Peng, 2008, p. 74)—arises in conversations. The double movement of the imagination produces both distance from the familiar (a space for thinking and seeing something a-new) and connectivity with the strange (through stories told from a plurality of perspectives). This work of distancing and bridging is typical not only of critical thinking, but also of creative processes (see Engels-Schwarzpaul, 2013, p. 167).
15. Strangely, Rancière insisted until recently that emancipation can only be an individual act but recently, he seems to open up to the possibility of including collective process in emancipation (Rancière, 2010, pp. 6, 16).
16. Thanks to Ross Jenner for his comments on the final draft and particularly for reminding me of Gadamer's remarks.
17. See note 3.

References

Arendt, H. (1998). *The human condition*. Chicago, IL: University of Chicago Press. Original work published 1958.
Arendt, H. (1961). The crisis in education. *Between past and future: Six exercises in political thought* (pp. 173–196). New York, NY: The Viking Press Inc.
Arendt, H. (1992). *Lectures on Kant's political philosophy. Edited and with an interpretive essay by Ronald Beiner*. Chicago, IL: The University of Chicago Press.
Baecker, D. (2012). *Wozu Kultur?* [Why culture?]. Berlin: Kadmos.
Barone, T. (2008). How arts-based research can change minds. In M. Cahnmann-Taylor, & R. Siegesmund (Eds.), *Arts-based research in education: Foundations for practice* (pp. 28–49). New York, NY: Routledge.
Beck, U., & Grande, E. (2010). Varieties of second modernity: The cosmopolitan turn in social and political theory and research. *The British Journal of Sociology, 61*, 409–443.
Benjamin, W. (1998). *Understanding Brecht* (A. Bostock, Trans.). London: Verso. Retrieved from /z-wcorg/database
Bentley, T. (1999). *Pakeha Maori. The extraordinary story of the Europeans who lived as Maori in early New Zealand*. Auckland: Penguin.
Bingham, C. W., Biesta, G., & Rancière, J. (2010). *Jacques Rancière: Education, truth, emancipation*. London: Continuum.
Chambers, S. A. (2012). Jacques Rancière's lesson on the lesson. *Educational Philosophy and Theory, 45*, 637–646.
Cunningham, C. (2011). Chapter 11: Adolescent development for Māori. In *Improving the transition. Reducing social and psychological morbidity during adolescence. A report from the Prime Minister's Chief Science Advisor* (pp. 145–152). Auckland: Office of the Prime Minister's Science Advisory Committee.
Curtis, K. (2001). Multicultural education and Arendtian conservatism: On memory, historical injury, and our sense of the common. In M. Gordon (Ed.), *Hannah Arendt and education: Renewing our common world* (pp. 127–152). Boulder, CO: Westview Press.
Dikeç, M. (2013). Beginners and equals: Political subjectivity in Arendt and Rancière. *Transactions of the Institute of British Geographers, 38*, 78–90.
Disch, L. J. (1994). *Hannah Arendt and the limits of philosophy*. Ithaka, NY: Cornell University.
Eiland, H., & Jennings, M. W. (2014). *Walter Benjamin: A critical life*. Cambridge, MA: Harvard University Press.

Emadi, A. (2014). *Motion within motion: Investigating digital video in light of substantial motion* (PhD). Auckland, NZ: Auckland University of Technology. Retrieved from http://aut.researchgateway.ac.nz/handle/10292/7932#fulltext

Engels-Schwarzpaul, A.-C. (2013). Emerging knowledge, translation of thought. In A.-C. Engels-Schwarzpaul & M. A. Peters (Eds.), *Of other thoughts: Non-traditional ways to the doctorate* (pp. 163–179). Rotterdam: Sense.

Engels-Schwarzpaul, A.-C., & Emadi, A. (2011). Thresholds as spaces of potentiality: Non-traditional PhD candidatures in art and design. *ACCESS critical perspectives on communication, cultural and policy studies, 30*(2), 1–14.

Gadamer, H.-G. (1975). *Truth and method*. New York, NY: The Continuum Publishing Corporation.

Gilroy, P. (2005). *Postcolonial melancholia*. New York, NY: Columbia University Press.

Goultschin, M. (2014). We who stand to differ: Hannah Arendt on maintaining otherness. *Atlantic Studies, 11*, 277–299.

Gunew, S. (2013). Estrangement as pedagogy. The cosmopolitan vernacular. In R. Braidotti, P. Hanafin, & B. Blaagaard (Eds.), *After cosmopolitanism* (pp. 265–297). Miton Park: Routledge/GlassHouse.

Halse, C. (2011). 'Becoming a supervisor': The impact of doctoral supervision on supervisors' learning. *Studies in Higher Education, 36*, 557–570.

Halse, C., & Bansel, P. (2012). The learning alliance: Ethics in doctoral supervision. *Oxford Review of Education, 38*, 377–392.

Head, L. F., & Mikaere, B. (1988). *Was 19th century Maori society literate? Archifacts*. Symposium conducted at the meeting of the Conference Papers: Off the Beaten Record (11th annual conference of the Archives and Records Association of New Zealand, Christchurch, 28–29 August 1987), Christchurch.

Ho, K. T. (2013). Transfer and translation: Negotiating conflicting worldviews. In A.-C. Engels-Schwarzpaul, & M. A. Peters (Eds.), *Of other thoughts: non-traditional ways to the doctorate* (pp. 83–99). Rotterdam: Sense.

Honig, B. (2006). Another cosmopolitanism? Law and politics in the new Europe. In S. Benhabib (Ed.), *Another cosmopolitanism* (pp. 103–127). Oxford: Oxford University Press.

Ings, W. (2013). Queer as a two-bob watch. In A.-C. Engels-Schwarzpaul, & M. A. Peters (Eds.), *Of other thoughts: Non-traditional ways to the doctorate* (pp. 131–146). Rotterdam: Sense.

Isenberg, B. (2012). Critique and crisis. Reinhart Koselleck's thesis of the genesis of modernity. *Eurozine-Network of European Cultural Journals*. Retrieved from http://www.eurozine.com/articles/2012-05-18-isenberg-en.html

Jenner, R. (2013). Thought out of bounds: Theory and practice in architecture doctorates. In A.-C. Engels-Schwarzpaul, & M. A. Peters (Eds.), *Of other thoughts: Non-traditional ways to the doctorate* (pp. 203–220). Rotterdam: Sense.

Lane, A. M. (1997). Books in review. *Political Theory, 25*, 137–159.

Manathunga, C. (2013). Culture as a place of thought: Supervising diverse candidates. In A.-C. Engels-Schwarzpaul, & M. A. Peters (Eds.), *Of other thoughts: Non-traditional ways to the doctorate* (pp. 67–82). Rotterdam: Sense.

Masschelein, J. (2011). Experimentum scholae: The world once more ... but not (Yet) finished. *Studies in Philosophy and Education, 30*, 529–535.

Mitra, S., & Dangwal, R. (2010). Limits to self-organising systems of learning—The Kalikuppam experiment. *British Journal of Educational Technology, 41*, 672–688.

Nepia, M. (2013a). Ruku – Dive. A physicality of thought. In A.-C. Engels-Schwarzpaul, & M. A. Peters (Eds.), *Of other thoughts: Non-traditional ways to the doctorate* (pp. 17–22). Rotterdam: Sense.

Nepia, P. M. (2013b). *Te Kore – Exploring the Māori concept of void* (Thesis, Doctor of Philosophy). Auckland University of Technology, Auckland, NZ. Retrieved from http://aut.researchgateway.ac.nz/handle/10292/5480

Pelletier, C. (2012). Review of Charles Bingham and Gert Biesta, Jacques Rancière: Education, truth, emancipation. *Studies in Philosophy and Education, 31*, 613–619.

Peng, Y. (2008). *A U-turn in the Desert: Figures and motifs of the Chinese nineteen eighties* (PhD). Minneapolis, MN, University of Minnesota.

Pesce, S. (2011). Institutional pedagogy and semiosis: Investigating the missing link between Peirce's semiotics and effective semiotics. *Educational Philosophy and Theory, 43*, 1145–1160.

Rancière, J. (1991). *The ignorant schoolmaster: Five lessons in intellectual emancipation* (K. Ross, Trans.). Stanford, CA: Stanford University Press.

Rancière, J. (2003). Comment and responses. *Theory & Event, 6*(4). Retrieved from http://muse.jhu.edu.ezproxy.aut.ac.nz/journals/theory_and_event/v006/6.4ranciere.html

Rancière, J. (2004). *The philosopher and his poor* (A. Parker, Trans.). Durham, NC: Duke University Press.

Rancière, J. (2010). On ignorant schoolmasters. In C.W. Bingham, & G. Biesta (Eds.), *Jacques Rancière: Education, truth, emancipation* (pp. 1–24). New York, NY: Continuum.

Rancière, J., & Stamp, R. (2011). Against an ebbing tide: An interview with Jacques Rancière (R. Stamp, Trans.). In *Reading Rancière. Critical Dissensus* (pp. 238–251). London: Continuum.

Ryan, Y., & Zuber-Skerritt, O. (1999). *Supervising postgraduates from non-English speaking backgrounds*. Maidenhead: Open University Press.

Schaap, A. (2011). Enacting the right to have rights: Jacques Ranciere's critique of Hannah Arendt. *European Journal of Political Theory, 10*, 22–45.

Singh, M., & Chen, X. (2011). Ignorance and pedagogies of intellectual equality. In A. Lee, & S. Danby (Eds.), *Reshaping doctoral education: International approaches and pedagogies* (pp. 187–203). Milton Park: Routledge.

Slee, J. (2010). A systemic approach to culturally responsive assessment practices and evaluation. *Higher Education Quarterly, 64*, 246–260.

Taylor, S., & Beasley, N. (2005). *A handbook for doctoral supervisors*. Milton Park: Routledge.

Todd, S. (2010). Living in a dissonant world: Toward an agonistic cosmopolitics for education. *Studies in Philosophy and Education, 29*, 213–228.

Actual Minds of Two Halves: Measurement, Metaphor and the Message

GEORGINA STEWART

Faculty of Education, The University of Auckland

Abstract

This article takes 'measurement' as a will to determine or fix space and time, which allows for a comparison of ontological models of space and time from Western and Māori traditions. The spirit of 'measurement' is concomitantly one of fixing meaning, which is suggested as the essence of the growth of the scientific genre of language that has taken place alongside the growth of science itself, since the European Enlightenment. 'Measurement' and 'metaphor' are posited as an original binary for classifying thinking and language, updating classical educational models of thought by drawing on recent results in brain and cognitive science, and recognising that basic cognitive resources, such as logic and rationality, power all forms of thinking. The article suggests that the notion of 'cultural worldview' may involve different balances of left and right brain thinking, embedded in the discourses, lexicons and grammars of each language, and that Western domination of left brain thinking (through the influence of science on the European languages, particularly English) may be a useful viewpoint on the philosophical dead end of the West.

Introduction: Mendeleyev's Dream and the Language of Science

A favourite story from science is that of Mendeleyev in 1869, working through a mid-winter's night in rural Russia (Strathern, 2000). His dream-inspired Periodic Table became the central concept marking the coming-of-age of chemistry as a discipline: an example of literacy of the highest order that allowed him to 'read' the very blueprint of matter, inaugurating the modern understanding of atomic structure.

An earlier version of this article was presented at the 43rd Conference of PESA (the Philosophy of Education Society of Australasia) held at the University of Melbourne, 2013, available at: http://pesa.org.au/images/papers/2013-papers/PESA_2013_Edited_Conference_Proceedings.pdf, pp. 184–191.

THE DILEMMA OF WESTERN PHILOSOPHY

Mendeleyev's genius demonstrates the closely intertwined nature of literacy and science, a connection obscured by recent educational trends to separate 'literacy' from 'language' in the notion of 'literacies'. The Periodic Table is an exemplar of the manifestation in science discourse of what might be termed the 'deterministic philosophy of measurement', a delineation of the contemporary concept of 'measurement', understood as exact determinations of some aspect of material reality, or space and time, which can be numerically or categorically represented.

Mendeleyev's dream is part of the story of the language of science, which is key within the overall development of modern science to its position today as the most powerful form of knowledge available to humanity, and a global network of complex social and technological systems and structures (Halliday, 2004). Over time, the interrelated development of science and modernity in post-Enlightenment Europe embedded this deterministic philosophy of measurement within language, especially English, which, for historically contingent reasons, has become globally dominant both as a world language (Crystal, 2003) and as a language of science (Ammon, 2001).

The language of science has been influential in all spheres, including the development of systematic approaches to education, and its subdisciplines of curriculum, pedagogy and assessment (Pinar, 2007). These recent fields are emerging at a time when educational discourses are dominated by a cluster of related concepts including evidence, standards, outcomes and accountability. These concepts share this underlying deterministic notion of 'measurement' as a fixing or specifying of some aspect of the phenomenon in question. The facile assumption that standardised testing is an objective way to 'measure' education reflects the influence of neoliberalism on education policy (Taubman, 2009). Thirty years of neoliberal reshaping of public policy and institutions have entrenched a culture of managerialism and technocratic approaches towards quality assurance, amongst other basic functions, in education systems (Pinar, 2012, Chapter 1: School Deform). Given the totalising nature of this neoliberal discourse, non-Western traditions such as Māori offer alternative visions and philosophies of what education, literacy, quality and equity might entail.

Binary Models of Thinking: Beyond Bruner in Educational Theory

A bipolar debate concerning 'indigenous science' and related questions features in the literatures on which educational research draws for its base of philosophy and theory. For example, the classical anthropological debate about 'rationality' posited science against indigenous knowledge, in efforts to clarify what science actually is, and how it works (Wilson, 1970). Second, the ongoing 'science wars' centre on the 'two cultures' in the academy, represented by the question of the status of social science, including education, as science (Sokal, 1996). Third, in work influential on educational theory, Bruner (1986) posited two basic modes of thought: 'narrative' and 'logico-scientific'.

Many such models of thinking have assigned *logic* to one side of the binary, thereby leaving it out of the other. Anthropology suggests logical coherence is characteristic of all cultural knowledge bases, Western and non-Western (e.g. Māori, see Salmond, 1985). But although Eurocentrism has been expelled from the academy, the association of science with modern Western culture as 'proof' that Euro-Americans are more 'advanced' than 'primitive races' remains a powerful 'subterranean' message in social discourse, retaining influence even within academia (Wetherell & Potter, 1992). It makes little sense to assign logic to 'scientific' thought, since narrative power also depends upon logical coherence.

The two modes of thought are perhaps better known today as 'left brain' and 'right brain' thinking (Lamb, 2004). As part of the biological heritage common to all human beings, the left brain/right brain model of thinking is more useful than Bruner's in domains such as science education, where Bruner's influence, one step from Eurocentric, is still evident in the dominant pedagogical metaphor that 'science is a special way of thinking'. Cognitive science and brain medicine have established that left brain thinking is typically analytical in nature, whilst right brain thinking is holistic. These two modes of thought are reflected in the two basic modes of language, here termed 'measurement' and 'metaphor'. This view sees logic as inherent in both modes of thinking and therefore in both modes of language. Not involving logic in the criteria by which to categorise modes of thought eases the longstanding debates about rationality, including multicultural science education research, epistemological diversity and incommensurability (Siegel, 2006).

Scientific English is a form of language that reflects the development of the modernist, deterministic philosophy of science. Science discourse requires that words and sentences have unambiguous meanings. Thus, though rich, messy stories from the history of science are preserved within science words, such as the names of the elements, in operation science language is profoundly nonmetaphorical: nouns, verbs and adjectives have stable, precisely defined meanings; and statements are intended to be understood literally, not metaphorically. Scientific English sacrifices richness of meaning in favour of precision: words and statements have single-layered meanings (not to be confused with the idea of simple vs. complex meanings). Importantly, this discussion refers to school textbook expositions of science knowledge, not the language of the world of 'working science' in practice. It is the textbook kind of science discourse that forms a sturdy 'gate' enacted in secondary science classrooms, which keeps most students, including almost all Māori, outside of that world of participation in science-related industries and professions.

Te reo Māori: Favouring Right Brain Thinking?

Speakers of Māori will immediately recognise that the above language descriptions are foreign, if not antithetical to the workings of te reo Māori. In contrast to scientific English, te reo Māori can be characterised as a language in which even very small words carry many levels and nuances of meaning, within an overall worldview built from the large tropes and metaphors of traditional Māori culture. The term 'worldview' is understood as a personal–cultural ontological, epistemological and ethical paradigm. Using in-depth investigations of both traditions and language features, Anne Salmond characterised the traditional Māori worldview as structured by a series of large interlocking bipolar opposites at many levels, from psychological to cosmic (e.g. ao/pō, ora/mate, tapu/noa, etc.).

Not only are Māori words and phrases multileveled in meaning, but a great deal of the meaning of Māori words and statements rests in exactly *how* they are said by the speaker. Thus oratory is far more important in Māori culture than in modern Western culture. Sacrificing precision for richness of meaning is associated with this performativity aspect of language in te reo Māori, which is absent from modern scientific English. The need to modernise te reo Māori for its survival has led to many arbitrary decisions in recent decades, 'fixing' the meaning of certain traditional Māori words by aligning them to English words, in ways that reflect dominant contemporary understandings, sometimes obscuring the original richness of imprecision (Mika, 2012). One way this 'richness of imprecision' works is when a Māori word takes two meanings seen in English as opposites, such as the example commonly cited in education: the word 'ako' can mean either 'to teach' or 'to learn'. The context (including nonlinguistic features such as performativity) determined which meaning was being invoked in any speech act. These differences and richness in meaning are not conveyed by the written words alone.

Perhaps traditional Māori language reflects a culture operating as much by metaphorical right brain thinking as the precise measurement left brain mode. Modern English is influenced by the scientific genre, reflecting the dominance of analytical left brain thinking, using precise, stable, literal meanings, which can be represented in written form without loss of content. In traditional Māori language, however, lexical words play a far lesser role in carrying meaning, which has more to do with how lexical words are arranged between many other small words. Over and above the words themselves, much of the meaning of a Māori utterance rests in the pacing and emphasis of each word, along with facial expression, gesture, and the use of other language devices, such as repetition, or extra nonlexical words added in for emphasis.

Another Look at Worldview and Epistemological Divergence

It is widely accepted that Western and Indigenous worldviews tend to be characterised by opposing binaries, but this does not make these ways of thinking mutually exclusive, in the sense of unable to be understood by someone brought up within the other culture or way of thinking. From the perspective of the modern scientific worldview, Māori knowledge has no explanatory power about the natural world. The scientific view is that Māori knowledge does exist in some scientific domains such as astronomy and taxonomy, arising from detailed observations of nature, but that this knowledge is a mere shadow of modern science knowledge in those areas. Science considers Māori knowledge to be underpinned not by working models of reality, but by 'stories'. The question of whether or not Māori knowledge is science (or a science, or antiscience) is really a question about how the word 'science' is being understood. Following the above argument, however, the value of Māori knowledge lies in it being *different* from science. My interest for some time has been in how to understand this undeniable difference, which is routinely experienced by Māori people, including myself, though denied by many scholars.

Might the concept of worldview, and the claims about epistemological diversity, be explainable in terms of (amongst other things) relative balance between these two modes of measurement (left brain) and metaphor (right brain) thinking? This idea follows Sydney Lamb (2004), who maps 'left brain' and 'right brain' thinking to 'philosophical differences' he terms 'splitter-thinking' (associated with absolutism, universalism and reductionism) and 'lumper-thinking' (associated with relativism and holism), respectively. A key Māori concept, namely 'whakapapa', may be used to explore this distinction. The dictionary translation of this important Māori word is 'genealogy' or 'family tree', but whakapapa is far more: it is a central trope in Māori cosmology, thought and knowledge, termed a 'cognitive gestalt' (Roberts et al., 2004); a 'way of thinking' (Barton, 1993, p. 59), 'both a noun and a verb' (McKinley, 2003, p. 21).

Amongst other uses, the whakapapa concept is also a record of the passage of time, based on the imprecise unit of a generation. In a society organised along communal kinship lines, knowledge of whakapapa was of both social and economic value. Whakapapa is usually portrayed diagrammatically using 'descending vertical lines', but Salmond's research showed that in traditional Māori thought, whakapapa was graphically represented in carvings 'as a double spiral marked by chevrons to show successive epochs' (1985, p. 247). If whakapapa measured time, the spiral representation of whakapapa reflects a Māori notion of time as cyclic, rather than the Western concept of linear time. A cyclic concept of time (such as the Mayan wheel of time) is a well-established characteristic distinguishing indigenous from Western thought. In Māori notions of space-time, the cosmic dualities (referred to above) are like the spokes of time's wheel.

Like whakapapa, the Periodic Table is also conventionally represented in linear form, with the elements arrayed in rows and columns. Yet before Mendeleyev's dream, in 1862, the French geologist Alexandre-Émile Béguyer de Chancourtois proposed the Telluric Helix model, with the elements arranged on a spiral line around a cylinder. Today, spiral representations of the Periodic Table abound, though not in science education. These two pairs of linear/spiral forms are possible examples of left brain/right brain representations. There is also a link with Robert 'Kaplan's Contrastive Rhetoric Doodles', a diagram first published in 1966, 'intended to demonstrate a variety of paragraph movements that exist in writing in different languages' in a article titled 'Cultural thought patterns in intercultural education' (Kaplan, 2005, p. 387). The Doodles diagram shows the patterns of English as a straight line, 'Oriental' as a spiral.

Conclusion: Implications for Intercultural Education

To think about recording whakapapa or the Periodic Table in spiral rather than linear form is like a thought experiment for better understanding the difference between left and right brain ways of conceptualising complex arrays of information. We can 'understand' how either representational form works; but few would independently think of transforming the conventional form of the Periodic Table, or common written forms of whakapapa, into a spiral-form representation. Lamb (2004) mapped each brain hemisphere to the various language functions taken care of by each side. This article applies Lamb's idea to the question of how left and right brain modes of thinking may work together, or in opposition, in representations of science—both in the characteristics of scientific English, and in 'school science'. The development of scientific English in the period of the European Enlightenment reflected an increasing relative importance of left brain or 'measurement' thinking, with burgeoning new technologies to observe nature to previously unimagined levels of precision, and concomitant relative decrease in language performativity, and other oral language functions aligned with right brain or 'metaphor' thinking.

In practice, of course, working science is highly diverse and multilingual; science relies on reciprocal relationships between metaphor and measurement, and on the engagement of all available cognitive resources. Scientific thinking cannot therefore be equated with left brain thinking, but this article suggests that science discourse, especially as presented in the school curriculum, may reflect a different relative balance, with more emphasis on left brain and less on right brain thinking, by comparison with the indigenous discourse of a non-Western culture such as Māori. It seems reasonable to suggest that this difference may contribute to the documented alienating effect of secondary science education on Māori and other indigenous or nonelite students, to a greater extent than for all students (Halliday, 1993).

In school science education and beyond, the characteristics of left brain thinking (as described by Lamb, above) have invalidly come to be identified with the nature of science, in a way that supports certain forms of scientism (i.e. ideological distortions of science) including the claims made by neoliberal economics to include 'scientific' approaches to social policy. The imbalance between 'measurement' and 'metaphor' modes of thinking and language seems characteristic of neoliberal discourse—lots of information but no wisdom; a checklist approach that misses the 'bigger picture'. The discourses, worldviews and epistemologies associated with indigenous cultural cosmologies, and the languages in which they are expressed, may differ most importantly from those of modern Western science in terms of this balance between the two great psychological modes of operation. This model supports the assertion of a coherent form of epistemological difference between 'Māori knowledge' and traditional curricular knowledge, whilst also clearly showing continuity between the two, and a way of explaining how the differences are not able to be captured in language by single words, but require exposition at the level of the paragraph, central metaphor, or discourse. The ideas brought together in this article suggest new approaches to future investigations into the role of language in science education for indigenous students, multicultural education, and intercultural studies more generally.

References

Ammon, U. (Ed.). (2001). *The dominance of English as a language of science*. Berlin: Mouton de Gruyer.

Barton, B. (1993). Ethnomathematics and its place in the classroom. In E. McKinley & P. Waiti (Eds.), *SAMEpapers 1993* (Vol. 1993, pp. 46–68). Hamilton: CSMER.

Bruner, J. (1986). *Actual minds, possible worlds*. Cambridge: Harvard University Press.

Crystal, D. (2003). *English as a Global Language* (2nd ed.). Cambridge: Cambridge University Press.

Halliday, M. A. K. (1993). Some grammatical problems in scientific English. In M. A. K. Halliday & J. R. Martin (Eds.), *Writing science: Literacy & discursive power* (pp. 69–85). London: Routledge.

Halliday, M. A. K. (2004). *The language of science*. London: Continuum.

Kaplan, R. B. (2005). Contrastive rhetorics. In E. Hinkel (Ed.), *Handbook of research in second language teaching and learning* (pp. 375–391). Mahwah: Lawrence Erlbaum.

Lamb, S. (2004). Philosophical differences and cognitive styles. In S. Lamb (Ed.), *Language and reality* (pp. 496–502). London: Continuum.

McKinley, E. (2003). *Brown bodies, white coats: Postcolonialism, Māori women and science* (Unpublished Doctor of Philosophy thesis). Hamilton: University of Waikato.

Mika, C. T. H. (2012). Overcoming 'being' in favour of knowledge: The fixing effect of 'mātauranga'. *Educational Philosophy and Theory, 44*, 1080–1092. doi:10.1111/j.1469-5812.2011.00771.x

Pinar, W. (Ed.). (2007). *Intellectual advancement through disciplinarity: Verticality and horizontality in curriculum studies*. Rotterdam: Sense.

Pinar, W. (2012). *What is curriculum theory?* New York, NY: Routledge.

Roberts, M., Haami, B. J. T. M., Benton, R., Satterfield, T., Finucane, M. L., Henare, M., & Henare, M. (2004). Whakapapa as a Māori mental construct: Some implications for the debate over genetic modification of organisms. *The Contemporary Pacific, 16*(1), 1–28.

Salmond, A. (1985). Māori epistemologies. In J. Overing (Ed.), *Reason and morality* (pp. 237–260). London: Tavistock Publications.

Siegel, H. (2006). Epistemological diversity and education research: Much ado about nothing much? *Educational Researcher, 35*, 3–12.

Sokal, A. D. (1996). Transgressing the boundaries: Toward a transformative hermeneutics of quantum gravity. *Social Text, 14*, 217–252.

Strathern, P. (2000). *Mendeleyev's dream: The quest for the elements*. New York, NY: St Martin's Press.

Taubman, P. (2009). *Teaching by numbers: Deconstructing the discourse of standards and accountability in education*. New York, NY: Routledge.

Wetherell, M., & Potter, J. (1992). *Mapping the language of racism: Discourse and the legitimation of exploitation*. New York, NY: Harvester Wheatsheaf.

Wilson, B. R. (Ed.). (1970). *Rationality*. Oxford: Basil Blackwell.

On the (Im)potentiality of an African Philosophy of Education to Disrupt Inhumanity

YUSEF WAGHID
Philosophy of Education, Stellenbosch University

Abstract

*Despite the advances made in the liberal Western philosophical and educational tradition to counteract unethical, immoral and inhumane acts committed by the human species, these acts of inhumanity persist. It would be inapt to apportion blame only to Western thinking, which has its roots in Greek antiquity, as Plato and Aristotle, for instance, perpetually and justifiably pursued and advocated the human enactment of civility and friendship in their writings. Instead of revisiting liberal views on education and arguing for a reconsidered view of humanityCPöa possible and plausible contentionCPöthis article draws on African philosophical thought on education to disturb some of the doubts in potentially disrupting atrocities committed against the human race, especially on the African continent. By drawing on the philosophical ideas of Agamben, in particular the notions of actuality, potentiality and becoming, it is argued that an instance of African philosophy of education—*ubuntu *(human interdependence and humanness)CPöcan do much to trouble the escalating levels of inhumanity on the African continent.*

Introduction

The idea that an African philosophy of education is not capable of counteracting inhumane acts, such as genocide, torture, murder and the abuse of human beings, has been dealt with extensively in previous works (Waghid, 2014; Waghid & Smeyers, 2012). The main argument has been in defence of the moral concept of *ubuntu* (human interdependence and humanness), as being capable of thwarting and even eradicating inhumanity as the continent battles the remnants of what is commonly known as the Arab Spring (peopleCPÖs revolt against unjust state rule in several northern African countries) in the form of persistent acts of hostility against humanity. This article takes a renewed look at African philosophy of education, without discounting the positive effects of *ubuntu* to resist inhumanity. It argues that *ubuntu* has to be considered always as a communal practice in becoming in order for the continent to disturb the tide of inhumanity that has swept unabatedly across the continent, and more people suffer the fate of extinction, torture and excommunication from their lands. Through the radical philosophical lens of Giorgio Agamben's negation politics, I argue that *ubuntu* has a more enduring potentiality to counteract violence if looked at in relation to the notion of a community in becoming. In doing so, I simultaneously dispel the notion that Western (continental) thinking has no relation to African thought and practice. Instead, practising a philosophy of education, more specifically of an African kind, invariably draws on seemingly incommensurable traditions to trouble the ubiquitous presence of inhumanity.

Inhumanity on the African Continent: A Persistent Violation of Human Dignity

Genocide on the African continent continues unabated. Whether in the form of atrocities committed by the Egyptian military rulers against protesting civilians, who insist in vain that the removal of democratically elected President Morsi be reversed; radical Egyptian Muslims desecrating churches and killing orthodox Coptic Christians; al-Shabab (the Youth) paramilitary forces massacring civilians in a Nairobi shopping mall; homophobic attacks against gays and lesbians by fundamentalist Muslims and Christians in Nigeria; Hutus raping and maiming women and children in the Democratic Republic of the Congo; Somali maritime piracy leading to assaults of members of shipping crews; and gunmen in South African township communities annihilating one another to gain more control over illegal drug trafficking—the inhumanity perpetrated against people on the African continent remains endless and horrifying. All the mentioned atrocities against humanity persist, despite African communities' apparent awareness that *ubuntu* should be actualised in their lived experiences, particularly in relations between individuals and others. *Ubuntu* (human interdependency) has been constitutive of African communal practices (and nowadays popularised through the media) for a very long time, to the extent that the practice has been linked to forms of communitarianism that should be actualised, such as having respect for elders, treating the destitute and helpless with care and cultivating sharing and trust amongst Africa's peoples (Waghid, 2014, pp. 58–62). One cannot deny the need for *ubuntu* to manifest itself in the practices of people, considering the escalating levels of human indignity that have become endemic in certain parts of African society. There are those critics of *ubuntu* who use the inhumanity that prevails in certain parts of the continent as reason to take issue with the practice, and even to question whether Africa has the moral commitment to remedy its own continuing societal demise. There are others who go so far as stating that *ubuntu* contributes towards Africa's moral malaise on account of its incipient potential to polarise communities along ethnically divisive understandings of *ubuntu*. Small wonder, then, that ethnic rivalries are so dominant and acrimonious in several parts of the African continent. I do not for a moment think that these criticisms are valid, as the ethical caring and compassionate mutuality associated with *ubuntu* make the practice an unlikely candidate for the discordant inhumanity some people suffer on the continent. For me, the answer lies perhaps in looking at *ubuntu* differently again—this time through the paradigmatic lens of the radical political theory of Agamben. It is Agamben's views on actuality, potentiality and becoming that will be used to reconsider *ubuntu* as a moral imperative for Africa to become more attentive to the inhumanity that has permeated several parts of the continent—a situation that affects all Africans, as well as those intent on seeing humanity holding sway on the continent, and everywhere else for that matter.

Potentiality and a Community in Becoming: Rethinking *Ubuntu* Again

As was mentioned earlier, *ubuntu* is a form of moral consciousness in terms of which communal Africans embark on caring, compassionate, hospitable and forgiving human engagements to ensure that human interdependency and humanity become actualised—that is, that they manifest in the practices of individuals and communities, including educational institutions (Waghid & Smeyers, 2012, pp. 13–15). At first glance, there seems to be very little wrong with arguing that acts of *ubuntu* should be actualised in communal practices so as to prevent human injustice. However, looking at the argument again, this might also be where the potential problem with *ubuntu* and its implementation lies. To assert that something is in actuality is to say that something has been exhausted in action and that there is no need for it to happen any longer, as its veracity is in the act itself. Simply put, having passed into actuality, *ubuntu* has no reason to happen again, as it is already with certainty in the practices of people. And perhaps this is the reason why people seem to be disinclined towards *ubuntu*, as it is erroneously assumed that the practice is already there in reality, yet interdependency and inhumanity are prevalent. Consequently, all enthusiasm for the practice is reduced when human indignity is observed, despite the apparent actuality of *ubuntu* in the lived experiences of some Africans. So, the question for me is not whether *ubuntu* is there (a matter of actualisation), but rather whether it 'can' be there. It is to such a discussion of whether something 'can' be there that I now turn.

Agamben (1999, p. 177) recounts the story of Anna Akhmatova, a gifted poet in the 1930s, who queued outside the prison of Leningrad with lots of other women trying to hear news of her son, who had been incarcerated as a political prisoner. On being asked by another woman whether she (Anna) 'can speak of this (situation)', Anna was reticent to respond until she said, 'yes I can'—that is, 'I can … [which] does not refer to any certainty or specific capacity but is nevertheless absolutely demanding … the hardest and bitterest possible: the experience of potentiality' (Agamben, 1999, p. 178). Although Anna could skilfully use language to tentatively describe the atrocities that happened to the prisoners, Agamben does not rule out the possibility that Anna might not actually be in a position also to describe the inhumane acts experienced by her son. In other words, for Agamben, the possibility that Anna can speak of atrocities is there, yet the possibility that she can also not speak of the atrocities is equally not there. That is, the potentiality that Anna can speak of atrocities and also not speak about them is always there. Drawing on Aristotle's idea of potentiality, Agamben (1999, p. 179) characterises two kinds of potentiality: generic potentiality, for example, a child has the potential to know or she can potentially become someone, and existing potentiality, in the sense that someone suffers an 'alteration' or 'becoming other'. So, whoever already possesses knowledge (who already knows) is not obliged to suffer an alteration, but those who do not already know can potentially come to know—a matter of becoming another. In this way, potentiality is not annulled in actuality, but remains conserved and 'saves itself in actuality', which, according to Agamben, 'survives actuality and in this way, *gives itself to itself*' (1999, p. 184). To come back to the practice of *ubuntu*, those who claim to have actualised *ubuntu* have not given itself to itself because *ubuntu* was annulled in its actuality. If *ubuntu* has been actualised, there is no reason why it should become, as it is already in actuality. Put differently, its potentiality to contribute to human beings becoming altered others will simply not be possible. This perhaps explains why human inhumanity is still prevalent on the African continent, despite claims that *ubuntu* has passed into actuality. The fact that it is perceived to be in actuality makes its potentiality an impossibility.

My interest in potentiality as contributing towards an altered other or a becoming other brings into play how individuals engage in community, in this instance in communal *ubuntu* (interdependent) practices. Agamben (1993, p. 86) argues for a conception of community that does not presuppose commonality or identity as a condition for belonging: 'Whatever singularities cannot form a *societas* because they do not possess any identity to vindicate nor any bond of belonging for which to seek recognition … the singularities form a community without affirming an identity, that humans cobelong without any representable condition of belonging (even in the form of a simple proposition)'. Agamben argues that a community of belonging is heralded in the event of Tiananmen Square, when thousands of Chinese students, workers and other protesters demonstrated against government corruption without clearly articulated demands taken on the basis of a 'common interest deriving from a shared identity' (Mills, 2008, p. 130). In the words of Agamben, '[w]hat was most striking about the demonstrations of the Chinese May was the relative absence of determinate contents in their demands (democracy and freedom are notions too generic and broadly defined to constitute the real object of a conflict, and the only concrete demand, the rehabilitation of Hu Yao-Bang, was immediately granted)'. Considering that the practice of *ubuntu* (human interdependence) has always been thought of as entailing communal practices, in which human beings share a common identity—ethnicity, culture and language—it follows that an Agamben perspective of *ubuntu* does not necessarily require humans to cobelong with reference to ethnic identity or ethnic difference. Communal *ubuntu* practices can still exist without appropriating a shared ethnic identity. In other words, Kenyan Kikuyus (the majority ethnic tribe) potentially can co-belong in community with minority ethnic groups, such as Merus or Kalenjins, without reference to their identities—that is, they can cobelong and thus peacefully coexist under conditions of humaneness and interdependence (*ubuntu*), without laying claims to the ethnic purity and language that often drive them apart. An *ubuntu* community in becoming exists in 'whatever being', in which singularity is no longer sequestered in a common identity. At once, 'I am because we are' (the common phrase in African communities to depict *ubuntu*) can potentially be 'I am because we can become [we are not yet]'. The political potency of such a view of *ubuntu* as a community in becoming can potentially disturb ethnic conflicts and clashes that often leave behind division, suspicion, destruction of the environment, loss of human life, homelessness, destitution, traumatisation, stigmatisation, stagnation of the education system, and hatred and anger amongst ethnic rivals (Nyakuri, 1997, p. 5). The fear ethnic rivals might have is that their culture, language and ethnicity will be sacrificed in the name of a common identity, often reflected in what the majority desires. In a way, an *ubuntu* community in becoming allows for a community of beings without identity. Such a community cobelongs without sharing a common identity, where the potentiality of inhumane treatment of the other remains in potentiality.

An *ubuntu* community in becoming is a 'community without presuppositions and without subjects [where different human beings are brought] into communication without the incommunicable' (Agamben, 1993, p. 65). When an *ubuntu* community in becoming is potentially brought into communication without the incommunicable, then the differences of language, of dialect, of ways of life, of character, of custom, and even the physical particularities of each, are brought into the open (Agamben, 1993, p. 63). This implies that such a community has nothing to hide and would not shame its individuals through arrogance and self-destruction. Such a community instigates its individuals to communicate that which might appear to be incommunicable. For example, the ongoing ethnic conflicts between rival tribes in several parts of Africa—commonly referred to as Africa's forever wars—are a sufficient justification for individuals to communicate the incommunicable. Gentleman (2010) is correct when he attributes Africa's bloodiest, most brutal ethnic wars that never seem to end to the combatants not having a common ideology or clear goals, or to the fact that they want to take over major cities:

> Today's rebels seem especially uninterested in winning converts, content instead to steal other people's children, stick Kalashnikovs or axes in their hands, and make them do the killing ... What we are seeing is the decline of the classic African liberation movement and the proliferation of something else—something wilder, messier, more violent, and harder to wrap our heads around. If you'd like to call this war, fine. But what is spreading across Africa like a viral pandemic is actually just opportunistic, heavily armed banditry ... I've witnessed up close—often way too close—how combat has morphed from soldier vs. soldier (now a rarity in Africa) to soldier vs. civilian. Most of today's African fighters are not rebels with a cause; they're predators. That's why we see stunning atrocities like eastern Congo's rape epidemic, where armed groups in recent years have sexually assaulted hundreds of thousands of women, often so sadistically that the victims are left incontinent for life. What is the military or political objective of ramming an assault rifle inside a woman and pulling the trigger? Terror has become an end, not just a means.

What is clear from the above depiction of ethnic conflict—terror—on the African continent is that the most obvious common interest that seems to perpetuate the ceaseless conflicts by mostly brainwashed child soldiers (boys and girls) 'who ransack villages and pounder newborn babies to death in wooden mortars' is crime and popular support (Gentleman, 2010). If the only proposed solution to the 'forever wars' is to capture with the prospect of prosecuting or killing the rebel leaders, then to my mind, there would not potentially be any end in sight for the violent conflicts, as violence only breeds violence, as Hannah Arendt (1969) reminds us.

It is here that I want to argue that ethnic conflict will remain in potentiality as long as an *ubuntu* community in belonging is not considered as a community that potentially can combat the violence under conditions of communication without the incommunicable. Ceaseless ethnic violence in the form of brutality, warfare, tyranny, rapes and murders can be considered as incommunicable acts of violence, especially when speech such as 'ramming an assault rifle inside a woman and pulling the trigger' is communicated. An *ubuntu* community in becoming potentially can engage warlords in communication without the incommunicable, because there is always the potentiality that ethnic conflict might be combated within its potentialities. What has emerged from the arguments in defence of an *ubuntu* community in becoming is that an instance of African philosophy of education—*ubuntu*CPöpotentially can undo the brutality and inhumanity associated with ethnic conflict and military coups on the African continent. Such a community in becoming potentially would offer more to combat the predatory style of warfare and conflict that has become endemic to African society. An *ubuntu* community in becoming seems to be AfricaCPÖs potential solution that can bring people from all spheres to cobelong as they set out to trouble the continentCPÖs conflicts that seem to remain in potentiality. Such a community would not predetermine who should be excluded, but rather consider each individual or group within its own singularity and potentiality worthy of engaging with, even if just on the basis of their being humans. Only through recognising that humans have the potentiality to communicate, without ending the communication on the basis of not using the incommunicable undignified, barbaric and brutal acts of violence to exclude perpetrators, the possibility is always there for the impotentiality of such heinous acts of savagery. This is not suggesting that perpetrators of brutal acts against humanity should not be reminded of their deeds. Rather, they should be (and potentially be prosecuted), but the heinous crimes should not be, a reason to prematurely exclude them from the act of communication, as this in itself potentially would not end the barbaric savagery. Put differently, people cannot show an unwillingness to communicate on the basis that the perpetrators of acts of brutality should be excluded. This is what an *ubuntu* community in becoming can do in both its potentiality and impotentiality. It is such a community that offers Africa hope to potentially bring its ethnic conflicts to an end, and if not, potentially so.

Now, considering that an *ubuntu* community in becoming is that community that has to advance African philosophy of education, it makes sense to integrate cultural understandings into reason-dependent practices in the educational curricula of Africans. This non-bifurcatory conception of education (culturally informed practices not being separated from reason-dependent action) has the potential to contribute towards the cultivation of AfricaCPÖs humanity, where an *ubuntu* community in becoming has a crucial role to play.

References

Agamben, G. (1993). *The coming community*. (M. Hardt, Trans.). Minneapolis, MN: Minneapolis University Press.
Agamben, G. (1999). *Potentialities: Collected essays in philosophy*. (D. Heller-Roazen, Trans.). Stanford, CA: Stanford University Press.
Arendt, H. (1969). *On violence*. London: Allen Lane the Penguin Press.
Gentleman, J. (2010). *AfricaCPÖs forever wars: Why the continentCPÖs conflicts never end*. Retrieved October 16, 2013, from http://www.foreignpolicy.com/articles/2010/02/22/africas_forever_wars
Mills, C. (2008). *The philosophy of Agamben*. Stocksfield: Acumen.
Nyakuri, B. (1997, February). *The impact of past and potential ethnic conflicts on KenyanCPÖs stability and development*. Paper prepared for the USAID Conference on Conflict Resolution in the Greater Horn of Africa, Nairobi: Department of History and Government, University of Nairobi.
Waghid, Y. (2014). *African philosophy of education reconsidered: On being human*. London: Routledge.
Waghid, Y., & Smeyers, P. (2012). Reconsidering *Ubuntu*: On the educational potential of a particular ethic of care. *Educational Philosophy and Theory, 44*(S2), 6–20.

Index

Note: Page numbers followed with "n" refer to endnotes.

Adorno, Theodor 47
African American philosophy 3
African-American philosophy: "Black philosophy" 25; conceptualization 21; dialectical thought 31; hermeneutic energies 31; non-Cartesian approach to 22, 26; normative assumptions 27; occidental philosophical practices 33; perennial assumptions 20; philosophical anthropology 31–2; self-other dialectic 24–5; social context 24; substitutability assumption 23
African communitarianism *see* Western individualism and African communitarianism
African philosophy of education 110–15
Aikenhead, Glen 42–3
Akhmatova, Anna 112
Allen, Anita 28–30
Althusser, Louis 7
Am Because We Are: Readings in Black Philosophy, I (Hord and Lee) 24–5
Arab Spring 110
Arendt, Hannah 88, 90, 91, 96, 98n1, 99n6–99n8, 99n12

Beaufret, Jean 7
Benjamin, Walter 88, 98n1
Birt, Robert 20
"Black philosophy" 25
Black Studies Programs 25
Buber, Martin 37, 38, 40
Butler, Broadus N. 28

Carr, Wilfred 49n2
cogito ergo sum (Descartes) 80

continental philosophy 15; and analytical philosophy 1
Critique of Pure Reason (Kant) 69, 70

de Chancourtois, Alexandre-Émile Béguyer 107
Descartes, René 22, 76, 80
Dirlik, Arif 47
Discipline and Punish (Foucault) 66
Discourse on Method (Descartes) 76, 80
Dorrian, Mark 99n9
Douglass, Frederick 20–1, 27
Du Bois, W. E. B. 29

Early German Romantics 15
Educating for Meaningful Lives (Webster) 83
educational agnosticism 84
Educational Philosophy and Theory 1
educational theory 104–5
Emadi, Azadeh 93, 96
Enlightenment and French Revolution 63
Enslin, Penny 2
epistemological diversity 106–7
'Existential is a humanism' (Sartre) 7

Fanon, Frantz 21, 24, 27, 31
fringe figures, émigrés and migrants: cosmopolitanism 88–9; Māori culture 88, 89, 92; non-traditional candidates 96–8, 99n5; pedagogies 91–6; resources and friendship 96–8; visibilities 89–91

Gadamer, Hans-Georg 97
Gay Science, The (Nietzsche) 8–9
Gordon, Lewis 28

Halse, Christine 99n11
Harris, Leonard 23, 32
Havis, Devonya N. 32
Horkheimer, Max 47

INDEX

Horsthemke, Kai 2
human freedom and philosophical attitude: challenging perspectives 62; cognitive science 62; conception of philosophy 65; contemporary conceptions 64; discipline of philosophy 65–6; educational disciplines 66; historical reflection 63; limitation 73n2; metaphysics and epistemology 63; relevance/irrelevance of 62–3; self-legislation/autonomy 67, 72; transcendental reflection 70–1, 72n1
humanist ideology: contemporary modern traditions 9; deconstruction 7–8; natural history 4; phallogocentrism 8; renaissance humanism 7; Smith, Justine E. 4–6
Husserl, Edmund 54

Ignorance and pedagogies of intellectual equality (Singh and Chen) 98n3
indigenous metaphysics 12–17
intercultural education, implications for 107–8
Invisible Man (Ellison) 26

Jacotot, Jean-Joseph 96
Johannes Climacus (Kierkegaard) 74, 82

Kantian critical philosophy 68–9
Kierkegaard, Soren 78, 84

Lamb, Sydney 107
Le Grange, Lesley 44–7
Letter on Humanism (Heidegger) 7
Lyotard, Jean-Francois 21

Māori culture 88, 89, 92, 105–6
Marks, Laura 93
Mavae and Tofiga: Spatial Exposition of Samoan Architecture (Refiti) 93–4
McLuhan, Marshall 55
Meditations on First Philosophy (Descartes) 22
Mendeleyev's dream 103–4
Meno (Plato) 75–6
Metz, Thaddeus 2
Mika, Carl 2
Mitra, Sugata 99n9
Mosley, Albert 29
Motion within motion: investigating digital video in light of Substantial Motion (Emadi) 93

Natanson, Maurice 25
Nepia, Moana 92–3, 98n3
Nietzsche, Friedrich 27
'non-Western philosophy' 4

Orientalism (Said) 45
Origins of Humanism, The (Mann) 6

Palmer, Fleur 94, 96
Papākainga development: Negotiating on contested ground (Palmer) 94
Peters, Michael A. 2
phallogocentrism 8
Phenomenology of Spirit (Hegel) 27
Philosophical Fragments (Kierkegaard) 74
Philosophical Investigations (Wittgenstein) 10n2
Philosophy Born of Struggle (Harris) 23
Piper, Adrian 30
Pippin, Robert 67–8
Principia Mathematica (Russell and Whitehead) 29

Rancière, Jacques 90, 91, 94, 98n1, 99n9, 99n12, 100n15
Refiti, Albert 93–4, 96
Remarks on Frazer's Golden Bough (Wittgenstein) 10n2
Renaissance humanism 7
Republic, The (Plato) 75
Rider, Sharon 2

Said, Edward 45, 47
Salmond, Anne 105
Sartre, Jean-Paul 22, 33
Sartwell, Crispin 22, 24
Scientific English 105
Scientific Revolution 12
Smith, Justine E. 4–6
Stewart, Georgina 3

Te Kore—Exploring the Māori concept of void (Nepia) 92
Telluric Helix model 107
Thomas, Laurence 28
Tragic Sense of Life, The (Unamuno) 78, 81

ubuntu community 111–15
Unamuno, Miguel de: certainty and doubt 77–8, 83–4; doubt, despair and hope 78–83; educational implications 80; 'tragic sense of life' 75

Waghid, Yusef 3
Wagner, Jon 44
Webster, Scott 83
Western and Indigenous worldviews 106–7

INDEX

Western culture, inherent dichotomy of 36–7; autonomy and affinity 40–1; dependence *vs.* independence 37–40

Western individualism and African communitarianism: *contra* 52; geographical labels 52–3; philosophy of education 53–7; political sensitivities 58n2; prima facie attractiveness 57–8

Western tradition: Aikenhead, Glen 42–3; colonialism's consequences 48; Enlightenment tradition 45; implications 47; implicit and explicit conversation 46; misconceptions and biases 43; overlapping 46–7; philosophical blindness 44–5

Wiredu, Kwasi 56

Yancy, George 3